John Daniel Walters

Projection Drawing

John Daniel Walters

Projection Drawing

ISBN/EAN: 9783743343412

Manufactured in Europe, USA, Canada, Australia, Japa

Cover: Foto ©ninafisch / pixelio.de

Manufactured and distributed by brebook publishing software
(www.brebook.com)

John Daniel Walters

Projection Drawing

WALTERS' ELEMENTARY GRAPHICS.

SECOND BOOK.

PROJECTION DRAWING.

BY JOHN DANIEL WALTERS, M. Sc.

PROFESSOR OF INDUSTRIAL ART AND DESIGNING IN THE KANSAS STATE
AGRICULTURAL COLLEGE.

MERCURY PUBLISHING HOUSE,
Manhattan, Kansas,

1894.

"*A place should also be found in the school or college course for at least the elements of the modern synthetic or projective geometry. It is astonishing that the subject should be so generally ignored, for mathematics offers nothing more attractive. It posesses the concreteness of the ancient geometry without the tedious particularity, and the power of analytical geometry without the reckoning, and by the beauty of its ideas and methods, illustrates the esthetic quality which is the charm of the higher mathematics, but which the elementary mathematics in general lacks.*"—*From the report of the committee on Secondary Studies, appointed at the meeting of the National Educational Association, July 9, 1892.*

PREFACE.

This course in **Elementary Graphics consists** of four separate text-books, each of **which** is intended to furnish daily work for a term of from **six to** twelve weeks, or its equivalent. It includes the subjects of

    1. Geometrical Drawing,

    2. Projection Drawing,

    3. Elements of Descriptive **Geometry**,

    4. **Linear** Perspective,

and was originally prepared for the classes of the Kansas State **Agricultural (and** Mechanical) College, but has been arranged here so that the different volumes may be used separately and under varying conditions. **It is** intended, however, that Geometrical Drawing should precede, and **Projection** Drawing should follow the study of Plane and Solid Geometry.

J. D. WALTERS.

Manhattan, **Kansas**, October, 1894.

GLOSSARY

OF MATHEMATICAL AND TECHNICAL TERMS.

The Numbers Refer to the Paragraphs Containing Definitions or Descriptive Statements.

Axial, non-axial................33
Axis of rotation..........13, 14, 15
Axonometry..................3, 31
Auxiliary plane................12
Auxiliary projection............12
Black printing 48
Blue printing...................48
Brilliant point 51
Brilliant line...........49, 50, 51
Cabinet perspective... 32
Conic section.....17, 18, 19, 20, 21
Co-ordinate...................19, 20
Co-ordinate planes.............12
Descriptive geometry......1, 2, 14
Dip............. 13
Directrix....................19, 20
Double curved surface.... 52
Development........ 24, 25, 26, 27
Elevation..........................7
Ellipse...................17, 18
Ellipsoid 29
False perspective..............32
Focus................17, 18, 19, 20
Generatrix........ .....18. 19, 20
Ground line.................. ..9
Helical.......................29
Helical flange. 29
Helicoid.... 29
Helix 28, 29, 30
Hyperbola 17, 20
Inking........ 47

Isometric.......3, 31, 35, 36, 37, 38
Light.... 39
Locus 17, 18, 19, 20
Major axis......................18
Minor axis......................18
Monodimetric........31, 32, 33, 34
Normal..... ....18, 19, 20
Ordinate 18, 19, 20
Orthogonal 3, 12
Orthographic 3
Parabola....................17, 17
Plan 9
Planes of projection..........6, 12
Plane of rotation...............13
Pitch..........................28
Projection 6
Rabattement 15, 22
Radius vector.........17, 18, 19, 20
Rotation. 13, 17
Scotia 54
Screw line..............28, 29, 32
Secant plane............ 15, 10
Section..........15, 16, 17
Serpentine......................37
Shades...... ....49, 50, 51, 52
Shadow 39, 40, 41, 42
Single curved surface...........49
Stippling 51
Torus 29
Trace..................12, 15, 12
Zincetching....................48

PART I.

Definitions, Problems and Exercises.

INTRODUCTION.

---

1. Projective Geometry.

The objects of projective geometry **are:**

(1.) To represent, by drawings, geometrical magnitudes in space.

(2.) To solve problems on forms in space by construction in a plane, and to demonstrate by the method of projections the properties of form and position.

Accordingly the subject matter of the science may **be divided into**

(1.) Projection Drawing

(2.) Descriptive Geometry.

2. Projection Drawing.

Projection drawing is the art of representing space **forms upon plain** surfaces, so as to show their real dimensions and relations.

Conceptions of the form of solids or objects having three dimensions, are at first obtained with difficulty from drawings. Especially is this the case when the drawings are not perspectives and lack shading. (Working drawings.) The systematic study of projection drawing is therefore a matter of great importance to everyone intending **to follow** an industrial, engineering or **artistic pursuit.** For the same reason, the study of descriptive geometry **is** usually preceded by a course upon the methods of representing objects **having** three dimensions. It is evident that **the** student must learn to read and draw the language of space forms before he can expect to make progress in the analysis or such forms, just as he had to learn reading and writing before he could commence the study of rhetoric or literature.

3. Different Methods of Projection.

There are at least four scientific methods of projection drawing:

(1.) Orthographic projection.

(2.) Axonometric projection.

(3.) Conical projection.

(4.) Spherical projection.

Each of these has characteristics that make it suitable for certain kinds of scientific or practical work. In mathematical and engineering drawing, the first, or orthographic method, is commonly used. This book treats orthographic and axonometric projection.

4. Method of Work.

Experience has proved that a series of problems of progressive difficulty, which, taken in their logical order, the student can master alone, or with little assistance on the part of the teacher, will accomplish the desired ends better than any other.

Some of the work in projection drawing offers better opportunity for artistic efforts, requires larger sheets of paper, and should be done under the eye of the teacher, while a majority of the problems may be solved on smaller sheets, simply with triangle and compasses. For this reason, this book, like Book 1, has been divided into two parts:

Part I.—Definitions, problems and exercises.

Part II.—Shading and draughting.

The first part contains the subject matter of the home work, and the second part that for the class room work. The study of both parts should be commenced at the same time, and should be carried on together. One day should be given to discussions and illustrations of new principles and to blackboard recitations by the class; the next day should be devoted to draughting in the class room.

Fig. 1.

All home work in projection drawing should be done in ink and should be finished uniformly, so as to permit binding at the close of the term. Each plate should be drawn with a heavy border line inclosing a surface of 6½ by 9 inches. Only one side of the paper should be used. The sheet should not be rolled, but ought to be carried "flat" in a large book or a portfolio. "What is worth doing at all is worth doing well!"

5. Tools and Materials.

The tools required for the home work in projection drawing are:

(1.) A pencil of rich quality and hardness that it will take and hold a fine point.

(2.) An eraser.

(3.) A pair of solid white metal compasses with pencil and pen attachment.

(4.) A drawing pen.

(5.) A drawing board, 12 to 14 inches by 20 to 22 inches, (see illustration.)

(6.) A small T-square.

(7.) A right angled isosceles triangle having sides of about 6 inches.

(8.) Four small white metal thumb tacks.

Of materials, will be needed a bottle of jet black writing ink—not writing fluid, as this would corrode the drawing pen—and about three dozen sheets of best American drawing paper, size 8½ by 11 inches. This paper is usually sold in sheets measuring 17 by 22 inches and has to be folded and cut. If the finished work is to be bound, larger sheets should be provided and the additional margin should be arranged for on the left side of each plate. Good grades of French linen paper will also be serviceable.

The additional tools and materials needed in shading and draughting are described in the Introduction of Part II of this book.

DIVISION B.

GENERAL PRINCIPLES.

6. The Planes of Projection.

The solid or object to be drawn is supposed to be placed above a horizontal and in front or a vertical plane. These planes are called the *planes of projection*.

FIG. 2.

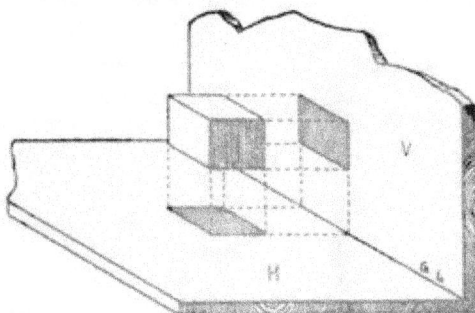

Perpendiculars, named *projectors*, are then supposed to be dropped from every corner or conspicuous point of the solid to both planes of projection. By connecting the ends of those projectors upon the planes of projections by lines that represent the edges or outlines of the solid, two pictures are obtained.

It will be seen that these pictures, named the *horizontal projection* and the *vertical projection*, form a perfect record of the solid or object, a record that enables the reader to imagine and measure the represented form.

In practical draughting, the horizontal projection is called *plan* and the vertical projection *elevation*.

A *plan* is a drawing made on a flat surface, which describes the length and breadth of a solid or object on a surface that is considered as always lying horizontal.

An *elevation* is a drawing made on a flat surface that is regarded as always standing vertical—perpendicular to the plan.

7. Plan and Elevation.

In figure 3, the student will recognize two vertical and two horizontal projections. i. e., the plans and elevations of a dog house. A careful study of all the features of this drawing will convince him of the facts stated in paragraph 6.

FIG. 3.

FRONT ELEVATION. SIDE ELEVATION.

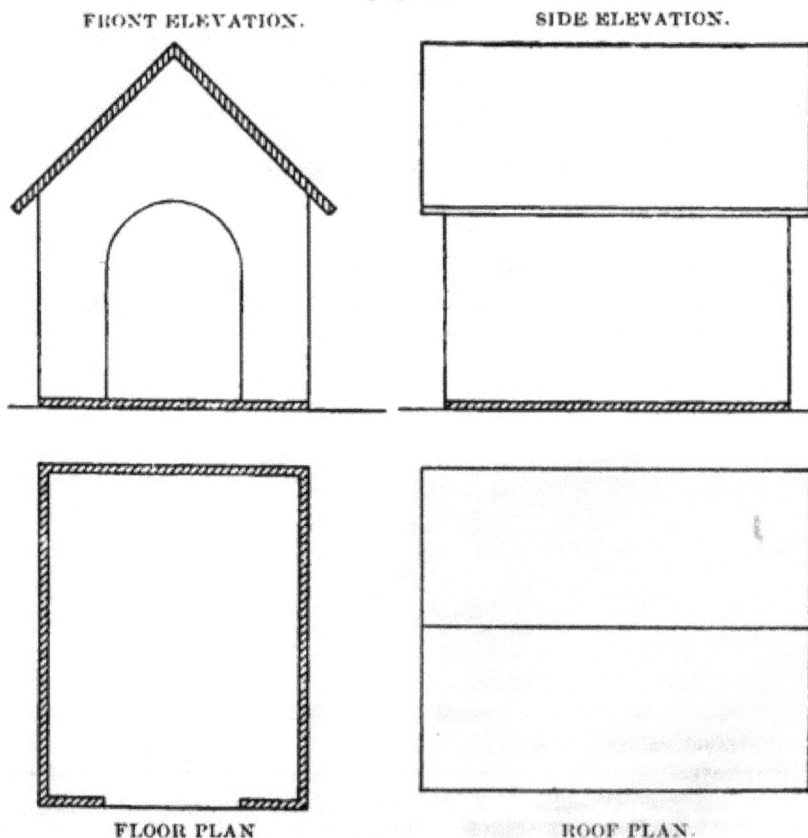

FLOOR PLAN ROOF PLAN.

SCALE 1 INCH TO 2 FEET.

A carpenter, asked so build a dog house like this, could go to work at once and construct it without asking a single question regarding its form. Understanding how to use the *scale of one inch to two feet*, which has been used in making this draught, he could measure the height of the whole object, the height of the sides and the height of the opening, in the two elevations, while he could obtain the horizontal measure, the thickness of the boards, etc., in the plans.

To read simple plans and elevations, like these, is not difficult, but there are many questions arising in connection with the drawing and reading of forms of three dimensions that will tax the student more severely. Everyone can read an item in a book or newspaper without much of an effort, yet few are able to write an article grammatically and rhetorically correct. In order to acquire the ability to do this, language must be studied systematically. The student must look for general *principles*.

8. Seven Principles.

From the given figures, and from blackboard drawings and models exhibited by the teacher, the following principles may readily be deduced:

(1) Two planes, at right angles to each other, are necessary to fully represent the three dimensions, length, width and height, of a solid.

(2) These two planes may really consist of one surface only. By dividing it, i. e., the sheet of paper, the slate, or the blackboard, by a horizontal line, we can readily imagine the upper part to be vertical and the lower part to be horizontal.

This horizontal division line is called the *ground line*.

(3.) In order that dimensions shall be seen in the projections in their true size and relative position, they must be parallel to that plane on which they are shown.

(4.) Each plane shows two of the dimensions of the solid—the two which are parallel to it.

(5.) The dimension which is shown twice, is the one which is parallel to both of the planes.

(6) The height of the vertical projection of a point above the ground line, is equal to the height of the point itself, in space, above the horizontal plane.

(7.) The perpendicular distance of the horizontal projection of a point from the ground line, is equal to the perpendicular distance of the point itself, in front of the vertical plane.

9. Examples and Problems.

Having established these principles, it should not be difficult to read the following figures and to construct the projections required in this paragraph.

Note that the *ground line* is marked G L and is drawn in full line, while the *projectors*, and the edges not seen from above and from the front, are drawn in dotted line. This should be done in all required work.

In projection drawing, *to draw* means to find the horizontal and vertical projection. All solids should be drawn with their axis in vertical position and standing upon H, unless otherwise specified.

PROBLEM 1. To draw the projections of a cube having edges of 2¾ inches.

PROBLEM 2. To draw a hexagonal prism having a base diagonal of 2¾ inches and an altitude of 3½ inches.

PROBLEM 3. To draw a pentagonal pyramid, 4 inches high; its base having sides of 1¼ inches.

PROBLEM 4. To draw a triangular pyramid, 4 inches high, with a base having sides of 2 inches. Represent it as standing upon its *apex*.

PROBLEM 5. To draw a cone with its axis horizontal and parallel to V; altitude 3 inches; diameter of base 3 inches.

FIG. 4.	FIG. 5.	FIG. 6.	FIG. 7.	FIG. 8.

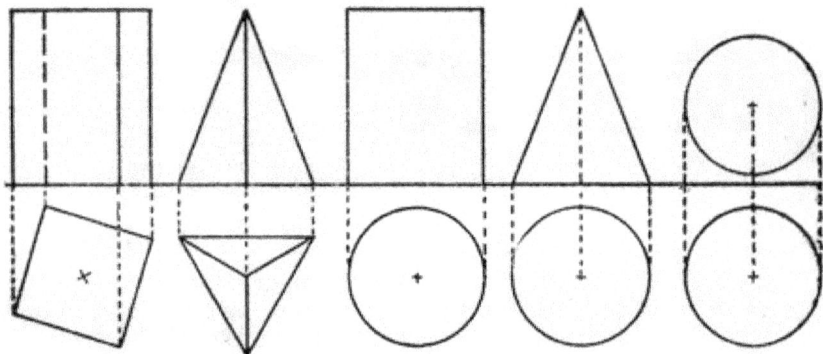

PROBLEM 6. To draw a sphere having a radius of 1¾ inches, and having its center 2 inches from both planes of projection.

PROBLEM 7. To draw the projections of a common thread spool, consisting of a cylindric shaft and two truncated cones, the whole pierced by a cylindric opening. Length of spool 3 inches, length of shaft 2 inches, diameter of shaft 1 inch, diameter of ends 2 inches, diameter of opening ¼ inch.

10. The Projection of the Straight Line.

From the last exercise the student has learned that a *line in space* can have four radically different positions with regard to the planes of projection. It may be

(1.) Parallel to both.
(2.) Parallel to one and perpendicular to the other.
(3.) Parallel to one and oblique to the other.
(4.) Oblique to both.

If the student will read figures 9-14 by illustrating them with his pencil as representing the line in space, using the table to represent H

and **a standing** book to represent V, he will notice that the **projection of
a line in space is** either

  (a) equal to the real line,
  (b) shorter than the real line, **or**
  (c) a point.

FIG. 9.   FIG. 10.   FIG. 11.   FIG. 12.   FIG. 13.   FIG. 14.

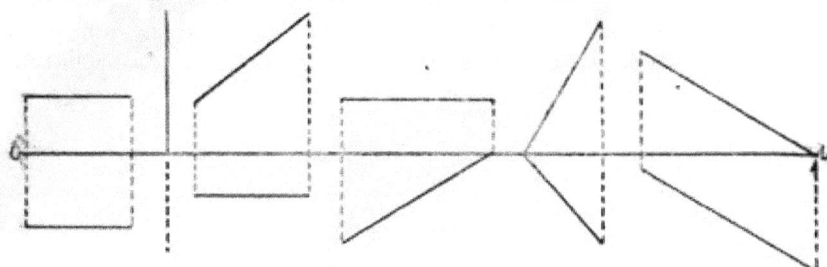

PROBLEM 8. To draw three lines parallel to H and V, two lines parallel to V and oblique to H, three lines oblique to H and V.

11. Mensuration of the Line in Space.

In the first three cases of paragraph 10, the line in space may be
measured *directly* by measuring one of its projections. In the fourth case
both projections are shorter than the real line and this can therefore **not**
be measured directly   The length must be found *indirectly*, which may be
done in several ways.

From the following figure it will appear that the line in space is the
hypotenuse of a triangle of which in every case the two sides are shown.

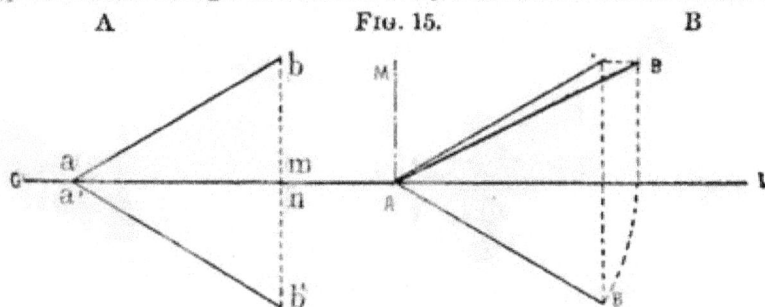

A   FIG. 15.   B

$$A B^2 = (a' b')^2 + (m\,b)^2$$
$$A B = \sqrt{(a' b')^2 + (m b)^2}$$

In construction, the real length of the line in space may be found by
rotation, i. e., by revolving it about a known *axis* until it becomes parallel
to either of the planes of projection.

In Fig. B, the **line A B** has been revolved about the vertical axis A
M into V, where it **now appears** at full length. The student will see, that

the line might have been revolved about a vertical axis through B, or a horizontal axis through A, or a horizontal axis through B, or in fact, about any vertical or horizontal axis in space. In every case there would have been the same result

The ability of revolving or rotating any line in space about any vertical or horizontal axis into a position parallel to V or H is very valuable and the student should execute such rotations until he becomes proficient, not only in measuring lines of all possible original positions, but also in imagining such rotations in space, without any drawing or experimenting.

DIVISION C.

AUXILIARY AND SECANT PLANES, ROTATION.

12. The Auxiliary Plane.

Figure 2 gives two elevations of a dog house. The first elevation represents the front and the second the side Most objects require two eleva-

Fig 16.

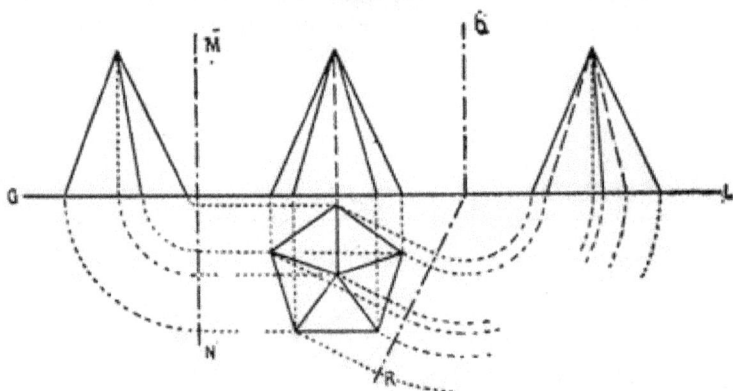

tions on two plans, i. e., they require an additional projection upon an *auxiliary plane of projection*. Such a plane is usually, though not always, a vertical plane placed perpendicular to the two main (co-ordinate) planes of projection to right or left of the object.

An examination of the above figure will show how an *auxiliary projection* may be obtained from the given main projections.

The dot and dash lines represent auxiliary planes of projection, i. e., they are the intersections (*traces*) of auxiliary planes with H or V (These two capital letters are common aoreviations for vertical plane of projection and horizontal plane of projection.)

After having drawn the projectors *orthogonal* (rectangular) to the auxiliary planes, these are *rotated* about their vertical traces into V (or H, as the case may be) and become a part of V. The arcs show the movement of the projections pending the *rotation*.

PROBLEM 10. To draw the horizontal and vertical projection of a vertical heptagonal prism and to find two auxiliary vertical projections.

Place the right auxiliary plane perpendicular to V and H, and the left auxiliary plane at 60° to V and 90° to H. Draw the figures so as to reasonably fill the space within the border line of the page (6¼ by 9 inches.) Draw all projectors in dotted line or full red ink; the auxiliary planes in black dot and dash line, the G L and the visible edges in the projections in strong black line; the rear or invisible edges in dotted black line

13. Vertical Rotation.

Instead of using the auxiliary plane to obtain additional projections, the object itself may be *revolved* or *rotated* so as to produce different projections upon V or H.

FIG. 17.

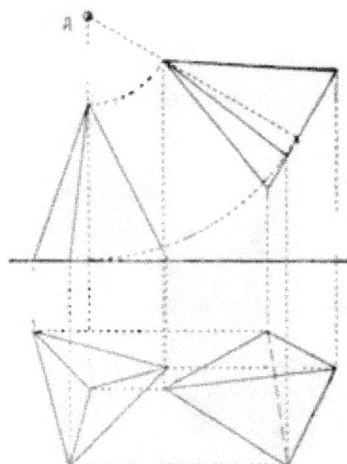

Figure 17 shows the rotation of a three-sided pyramid about an *imaginary axis*. The axis is a line perpendicular to V through point A. The *plane of rotation* is parallel to V. All points of the pyramid move in arcs which record as arcs in V, and as straight lines parallel to G L in H. As a result a second vertical projection is obtained which is equal to the first, but has a different dip to H: and a second horizontal projection which is entirely different from the first, but shows every point at an unchanged distance from V

Solve the following problem:

PROBLEM 11. To rotate a vertical pentagonal pyramid through an angle of 30°; the rotation to be parallel to V and the axis of rotation to be ½ inch above the apex.

14. Horizontal Rotation.

In the last paragraph the solids were rotated about *horizontal axes*. This paragraph treats the rotation of single solids about **vertical axes**.

FIG. 18.

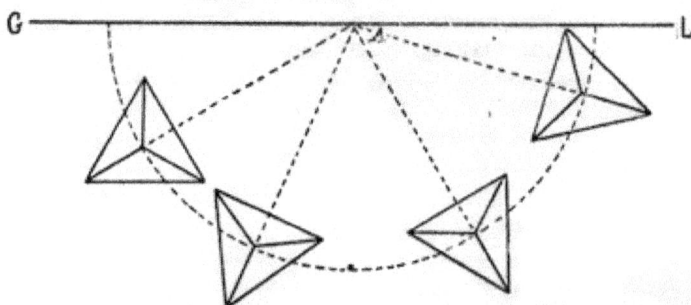

PROBLEM 12. To find the projections of a three-sided pyramid having a base edge of 2 inches and an altitude of 3 inches. The solid is to be drawn in four positions pending a rotation about a vertical axis, as indicated in figure 18.

Solve the following problem:

PROBLEM 13. To find the projections of a cube having an edge of 2¼ inches, in four positions pending a rotation about a vertical axis placed in front of the solid.

FIG. 19.

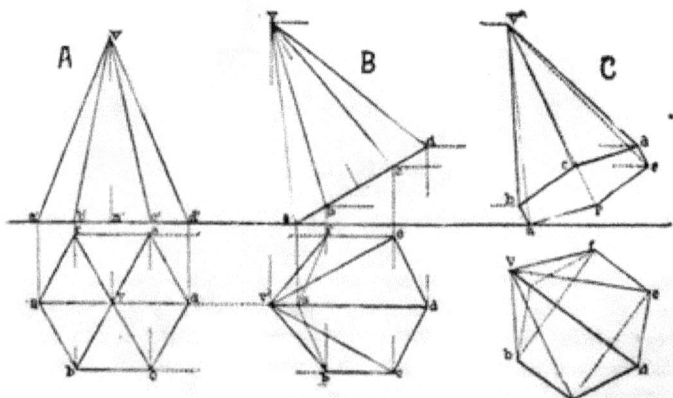

PROBLEM 14. To find the projections of a right hexagonal pyramid 2½ inches high and 1¾ inches in diameter at its base, whose axis shall be oblique to both planes of projection.

The **given** illustration represents the method usually followed in **placing** an object in an oblique position to both planes, though *descriptive geometry* gives additional solutions which will be explained in Book III **of this** series. Figure A represents the pyramid standing on H and par-**allel to** V. Figure B represents it tipped up and back to the left, and moved forward parallel to V, s, that every point in it remains the same distance as before from V. The vertical projection remains the same, except that it is oblique to G L. The horizontal projection is changed, and can be found by drawing projectors and parallels. Figure C repre-sents the pyramid, as it is in its second position, revolved 45° **about a** vertical axis of rotation. This places the axis of the pyramid **in the re-**quired position oblique to both planes of projection. The plan **in figure** C is the same as that of figure B, but the vertical projection **is** changed. It **can be** found by drawing projectors from the third **plan and** parallels **to G L from** the second elevation.

FIG. 20.

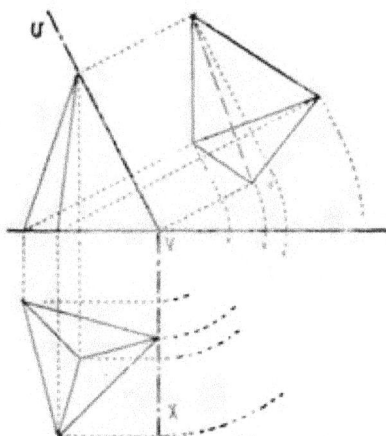

Solve the following problem:

PROBLEM 15. To **draw** a *plinth* (a low square prism). first, as lying upon H; second, as **having** been pushed to the right a distance equal to its length, and rotated 45° about a horizontal axis; third, as having been pushed to the right once more and rotated 30° about a vertical axis. Di-mensions 1 by 2½ by 2½ inches.

In Fig. 17, an auxiliary plane, U V X, has been placed oblique to H **and** perpendicular to V, so as to coincide with one of the slanting edges **of the** pyramid. As a result, the student will notice an additional pro-jection **to** the right of the main vertical projection. How has it been ob-tained? Has the oblique plane of projection been rotated about an axis? Can you illustrate the movement by means of models, i. e., a solid **and a** plane?

It is frequently required to lay a pyramid or other object having faces oblique to the axis, so upon H that it will appear to rest upon one of them. The problem can be rapidly solved by this method.

15. The Secant Plane.

A *secant plane* is an imaginary plane passing through a solid or object and cutting it into two parts. The imaginary cut or surface is called *section*. According to the position of the secant plane the cut may give a horizontal section, a vertical section or an oblique section.

The secant plane, like the auxiliary, is usually represented by its *traces*, i. e., its intersections with II and V. The traces are drawn in lines consisting of dots and long dashes.

Figure 21 represents a hexagonal prism cut by a secant plane which forms an angle of 45° with II, and of 90° with V. The section is evidently an irregular hexagon, the real form of which is found by its rotation of 45° about a horizontal axis of rotation through A and perpendicular to G L. The study of the given figure will explain the method and reveal the real form.

FIG. 21.

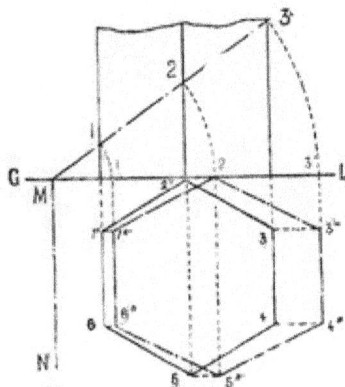

The rotation of a plane figure in space into a plane of projection is called *rabattement*.

Solve the following problem:

PROBLEM 16. To find the real form of the section of a given triangular pyramid, produced by a secant plane forming an angle of 90° to the left and passing through the right base corner.

16. Sections of an Irregular Pentagonal Prism.

Draw the projections of an irregular pentagonal prism resting with one of its faces upon II and having its axis parallel to V. To the left place an auxiliary plane perpendicular to G L. Upon this find the auxiliary vertical projection. The figure is now ready for the following problem.

PROBLEM 17. To find the real form of three characteristic sections of an irregular pentagonal prism, produced by three intersecting planes which intersect each other in a line in H and perpendicular to G L. One section is to be a triangle, one an irregular pentagon, and one a trapezium.

There are really four characteristic sections of this prism, the fourth being a rectangle. The student will readily see where and how the fourth section may be obtained.

DIVISION D.

PROJECTIONS AND SECTIONS OF THE CYLINDER AND CONE.

17. The Conic Sections.

The cylinder and the cone are closely related solids. In higher mathematics the first is considered as being only a special form of the second, i. e., the cylinder is defined as being a cone having an infinitely extended axis. For this reason the cone will form the chief object of study of this division.

FIG. 22.

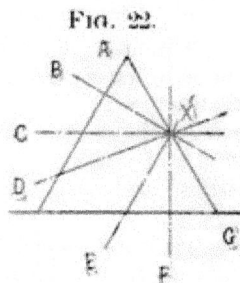

Figure 22 gives the vertical projection of a vertical cone. It also shows the *traces* upon V and through the cone of a *secant plane* in seven different positions. Every one of these *sections* differs from every other, yet they are evidently related to each other, because it can easily be shown how by rotation of the intersecting plane each becomes the other six by gradual changes.

At X assume an axis of rotation, perpendicular to V. Then let the intersecting plane rotate on this from position A through B, C, D, E, F to G.

The section at A will be a straight line.

The section at B will be an ellipse.

The section at C will be a circle.

The section at D will be an ellipse.

The section at E will be a parabola.

The section at F will be an hyperbola.

The section at G will be a straight line.

The sections at any place between A and C, and between C and E, will be ellipses; and the sections between E and G, hyperbolas.

The figure shows how the line, an element of the cone at A, is transformed into the other 4 forms—the *circle*, the *ellipse*, the *parabola* and the *hyperbola*—and how the last of these forms again becomes a line as the plane is rotated out of the cone at G.

By moving point X, together with the intersecting planes A, B, C, D, E, F and G, toward the apex of the cone, another interesting transformation takes place, which culminates, when this point is reached, into the following series of real or imaginary limiting forms:

The circle becomes a point.

The ellipse becomes a point.

The parabola becomes an element.

The hyperbola becomes an isoceles triangle.

By extending the axis of the cone, the parabola and hyperbola gradually approach each other and finally merge into the same limiting form. Both branches of both curves become one cylinder element.

A contraction (shortening) of the axis of the cone causes the section curves in space to gradually approach their horizontal projections, until the limiting form of the hyperbola, the straight line (chord), is reached.

The student should convince himself of these interesting relations of the different sections of the cone by carefully experimenting with a large cone, upon the curved surface of which he should draw crayon lines representing the sections named in this paragraph. He should make an effort to imagine the horizontal and vertical projections of these sections by looking at the model from different positions, and should familiarize himself with the names.

The conic section curves appear also as loci apart from the cone, but the cone is the most convenient form to observe their relation to each other.

In order to study the mathematical character of these figures or sections, it will be well to take them up separately, leaving out the circle, which has been studied to some extent in plain and solid geometry.

18. The Ellipse.

If a point moves in such a manner that the sum of its distances from two fixed points (foci) is constant, the locus traced by the moving point is an *ellipse*.

Figure 23 illustrates this definition and shows how, by means of two pins, a string and a pencil, an ellipse may be drawn.

The ellipse has two *foci* at A and B. It is a *symmetrical* curve about two lines, one of which is called *major axis* and contains the foci, and another, which is called the *conjugate or minor axis*. The axes are mutually perpendicular and bisect each other. The extremities of the major axis are called *vertices*. Any line from a focus to the ellipse is called *radius vector*. Any line perpendicular to the major axis is called *ordinate*. A *tangent* to an ellipse touches but does not cut the curve. A *normal* is a perpendicular to a tangent at the point of contact; it bisects the angle formed by the radii. The sum of the radii vector of the moving point in every position is equal to the major axis.

FIG. 23.　　　　　　　　FIG. 24.

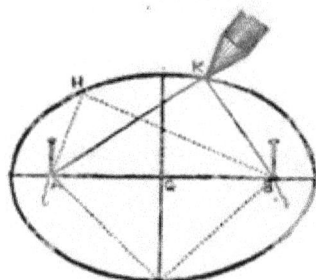 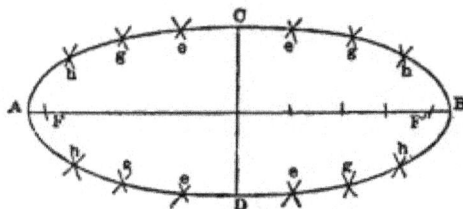

PROBLEM 17. (Figs. 23 and 24.) To construct an ellipse.

(1)　its major axis and one focus, or
(2)　its major and minor axis, or
(3)　its minor axis and one focus. or
(4)　its two axes, or
(5)　its two foci and one point in the ellipse being given.

The given definition and statements of mathematical qualities of the ellipse show that the problem is really the same in all five cases. In all cases it is necessary to find first the two foci and the length of the major axis, i. e., the sum of the *focal distances*.

After having found the foci and the major axis, the problem may be solved either with the string or the compasses.

In figure 23, pins are inserted at the foci and a string or a thread is tied there, equal in length, between the pins, to the major axis, or, which is the same, reaching from one focus to the extremity of the minor axis and back to the other focus. The inserted pencil will then describe the required locus.

In figure 24, the major axis is cut at random as shown. With A 1, A 2, A 3, as the radii and F and F' as centers. arcs are described in each quadrant. With B 1, B 2, B 3, etc., as the radii, and F and F' as centers, these arcs are intersected. A free-hand curve drawn through the points of intersection will be the required ellipse.

There are many other methods of constructing the ellipse. Some of these are simple, (compare figures 30, 32, 48, 49 and 59) and others are complex, but all involve the knowledge of some branch of *analytic*, or *projective* geometry, which the student may not have studied.

19 The Parabola.

The *parabola* is a curve which at all points, is equally distant from a fixed point (*focus*,) and from a fixed straight line (*directrix*.) Figure 25 represents a parabola with the directrix (M N,) the focus (F,) the axis, an ordinate, three radii, three co-ordinates, a tangent, a normal, and a chord.

Find these lines and note that the radius vector of every point in the curve is equal to the co-ordinate of the same point.

The parabola is sometimes defined as an infinitely long ellipse. Fig. 22 shows how by gradual change of the angle, which the intersecting plane forms with the axis of the cone, the elliptic section becomes longer until the parabola is approached. The ellipse intersects all elements of the cones of which it is a section. The parabola intersects all elements except one—the one which is parallel to it.

The circle may be considered as one limiting form of the ellipse, the parabola as a second, and the straight line as a third.

FIG. 25.   FIG. 26.

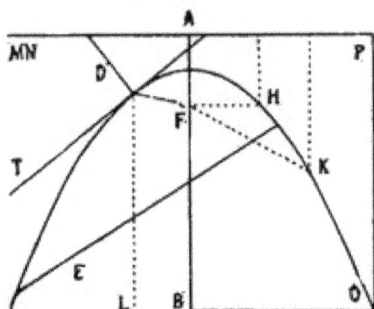

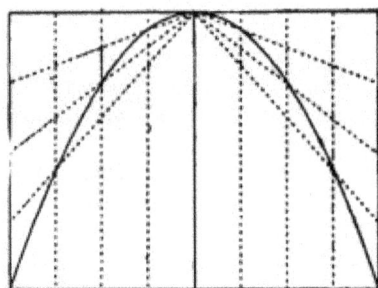

PROBLEM 18. (Fig. 25) Given, the directrix and focus, to describe the curve of a parabola.

Assume a directrix M N and a focus F. Draw the axis perpendicular to the directrix. Bisect F A. This is evidently a point in the curve, being equidistant from directrix and focus. Next draw a series of indefinite ordinates, on both sides of the axis, and find points upon them in the following manner: Measure 1 A and with the focus as center, cut the ordinate in I1. Then the distance of F I1 is equal to the distance from I1 to the directrix. It is therefore a point in the required curve. In a similar manner, a series of additional points may be found, which, connected by a free-hand curve, will give the required parabola.

PROBLEM 19. (Fig. 26) To inscribe a **parabola within a given rect-angle.**

The figure shows that the parabola **consists of diagonals in the trapezoids** formed within the given rectangle by **the two sets of connecting lines.**

20. The Hyperbola,

If a point moves in **such a manner that its** distance from **a fixed point** is always greater than its perpendicular distance from a fixed straight line, in a **constant ratio,** the curve traced by the moving point **is an** *hyperbola.*

The fixed point is the *focus,* and the fixed straight **line is the** *directrix.*

In **other words, an** hyperbola is a curve **that is** equidistant **at every** point **from two** unequal circles. See figure 28

The properties and functions of the hyperbola are **similar to those of the ellipse and the parabala.**

FIG. 27.   FIG. 28.

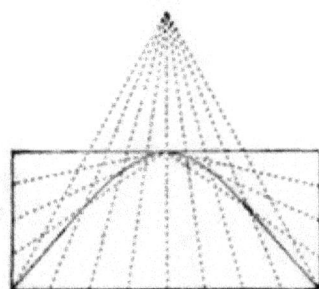 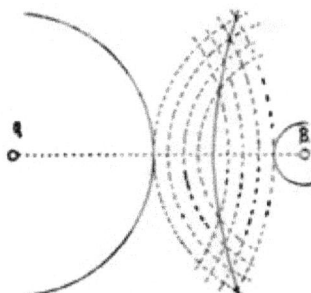

PROBLEM. 20. To inscribe an hyperbola within a given **rectangle.**

The solution **will** be plain from a study of figure 27.

PROBLEM 21. **To draw a plane** curve equidistant from **two given** circles.

The solution will **be apparent from figure 28.**

21. Projection of **the Circle, the Cylinder and the Cone.**

A circle may assume four radically different positions to the planes of projection. It may be

(1.) Perpendicular to both.

(2.) Perpendicular to one and parallel to the other.

(3.) Perpendicular to one and oblique to the other.

(4.) Oblique to both.

In case (1) **both projections are straight lines.**

In case (2) one projection is a line and the other a circle.

In case (3) one projection is a line and the other an ellipse.

In case (4) both projections are ellipses.

In all cases the greatest length of the projection is equal to the diameter of the represented circle, because in every position of the circle one of its diameters must be parallel to each plane of projection.

If the projection is an ellipse, the length of the minor axis depends on the angle which the plane of the circle in space forms with the plane of projection. In case (4) the minor axes of the two ellipses may be, but are not necessarily, equal.

FIG. 29.

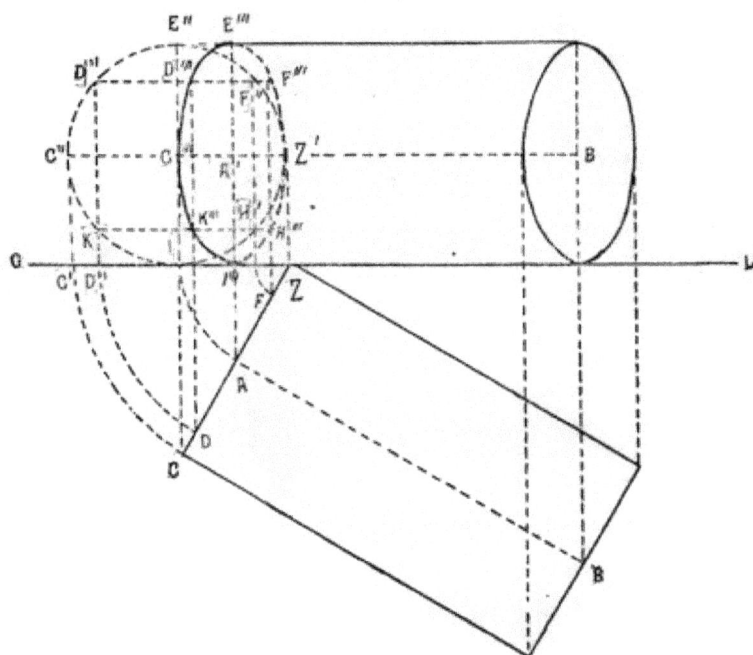

Having thoroughly comprehended these elementary principles, and illustrated every case by means of a circular disc and two coordinate planes, the projection of the cylinder and cone should not be difficult. Figure 29 represents a horizontal cylinder lying upon H, with its axis oblique to V. This horizontal projection is a rectangle, and must be drawn first. The vertical projection is obtained from the horizontal projection as follows: Project the centers of the circles into V and draw the top element. The end circles of the cylinder will appear as two equal ellipses in V. Find their axes by drawing the necessary projectors. Having found these, the ellipses may be drawn as shown in figure 23 or 24.

Another method consists in rotating the rear circle into V, about a vertical **axis Z,** marking a number of points in it as C, D, E and F.and revolving it back again to C Z. Pending this revolution, or *counter rotation*, as it is called, each point, except Z, describes a horizontal arc in space, which can easily be drawn in H and V. Parallels to G L and projectors will give the positions of the marked points in the required vertical projections. The outline is drawn freehand through the established points. The ellipse representing the front circle can be be drawn in the same manner.

The student will recognize in this work a method of constructing an ellipse of given dimensions.

Solve the following problems:

PROBLEM 22. To find the projections of a cylinder oblique to H and parallel to V.

PROBLEM 23. To find the projections of a cylinder of given dimensions, oblique to both planes of projections.

The problem is to be solved like problem 15, figure 20.

22. The Elliptic Section of the Cylinder and Cone.

The study of figures 30 and 31, which illustrate two simple methods of obtaining the real form of elliptic sections of the cylinder, ought to be sufficient to enable the student to find the real form of elliptic sections of the cone also.

FIG 30	FIG. 31.

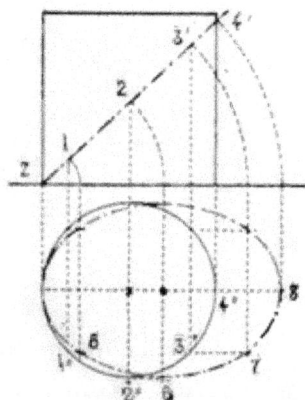 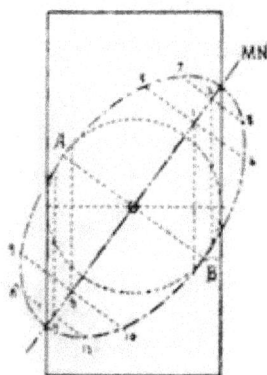

The first method rotates the intersecting plane into H and obtains the required ellipse as as a horizontal projection. The rotation is like that of figures 21 and 29 and is called *rabattement*.

The second method rotates the ellipse on its major axis into V. The *ordinates*, i. e., the perpendiculars to the major axis are obtained by measuring the chords in the horizontal section which is a circle.

Solve the following problems:

PROBLEM 24. Find the horizontal projection and the real form of an elliptic section of a given cone. The real form is to be found by the first method.

PROBLEM 25. Find the horizontal projection and the real form of an elliptic section of a given cone. The real form is to be found by the second method.

23. Parabolic and Hyperbolic Sections.

Both sections are frequently met with in mechanical work; it is impossible, however, to learn to draw them correctly and rapidly in all different positions without the knowledge of *analytic geometry*, which teaches their mathematical properties and relations as plain geometry teaches the properties and relations of the circle. No student who would master drawing can afford to neglect the study of this highly important branch of mathematics.

FIG. 32.

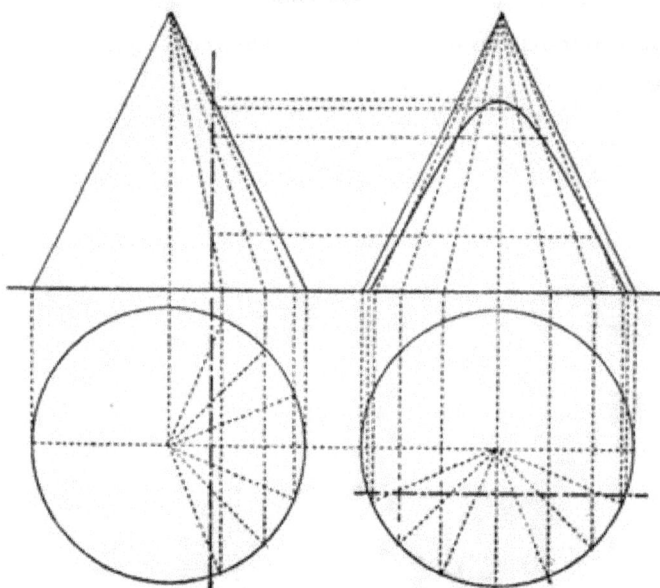

Figure 32 shows how to find an hyperbola from its given projections. The cone is posed so that both projections of the section are straight lines. The drawing of a number of *elements* will locate points that can be determined in all required positions.

Solve the following problems:

PROBLEM 26. Given the projections of a cone and the horizontal projection of an hyperbolic section, to find the vertical projection and the real form of the section.

PROBLEM 27. Given the vertical projection of a cone and the vertical projection of a parabolic section, to find the horizontal projection of the cone and the parabola, and to find the real form of the parabola.

PROBLEM 28   Given the vertical projection of a cone with the vertical projection of a parabolic section, to find the vertical projection after a rotation of 45° about the axis of the cone.

DIVISION E.

DEVELOPMENT OF SURFACES.

24   The Development of Rectilinear Surfaces.

If a surface of a geometric solid be rolled upon a plane so as to bring each consecutive face, or each consecutive element if the solid is a single curved surface, in contact with that plane without stretching, folding or tearing the face or element, the surface is said to be *developed*, and the plane figure which results therefrom is termed its *development*.

The cube, the rectangular block, the prism, the pyramid, and all polyhedrons are developable.

Figures 33 and 34 represent the developed surface of a right hexagonal prism and a right hexagonal pyramid, and explain how the development has been obtained.

FIG. 33.   FIG. 34.

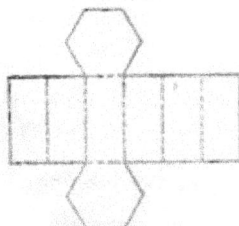 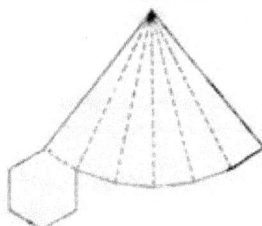

Solve the following problems: ·

PROBLEM 29.   To find the development of a cube having a right square pyramid upon two opposite faces.

PROBLEM 30.   To find the development of a truncated pentagonal pyramid.

PROBLEM 31.   To find the development of a cube cut into halves by any oblique plane, and having sides of 1 inch.

PROBLEM 32.   To find the development of a tetrahedron.

PROBLEM 33. To find the development of an octahedron.

25. The Development of the Cylinder.

The *development* of a right cylinder is an oblong or square, having a height equal to the axis or an element, and a base equal to the circumference. In practical work of ordinary character the circumference is usually measured by dividing the base circle into twelve equal parts and measuring the chord of such an arc of 30° twelve times. The resulting perimeter is, of course, slightly less than the circumference, because the chord is shorter than its arc.

In plane geometry the student has learned that the ratio of the diameter of the circumscribed circle to the perimeter of the inscribed dodecagon is 1 : 3.1058.., while the ratio of the diameter to the circle is 1 : 3.1416.. The above method of approximation is, therefore, nearly correct.

Solve the following problem:

PROBLEM 34. To find the development of a cylinder having an axis of 3 inches and a diameter of 2½ inches.

PROBLEM 35. To find the development of a rectangular stove-pipe elbow consisting of two equal pieces of sheet iron Length of axis of each part, 24 inches; diameter of pipe, 8 inches; scale, 1 inch to 4 inches.

NOTE.—The tinsmith cuts both parts out of one piece of sheet iron measuring about 26 by 48 inches. How can he do this ?

26 The Development of the Cone.

The development of the curved surface of a cone is a *sector*.

Solve the following problems for which no figures or solutions are given:

PROBLEM 36. To draw the patterns required by the tinner in making a *funnel* consisting of a combination of two truncated cones. Axis of large cone, 4 inches; axis of small cone, 3 inches; diameters of large cone, 5 inches and 1 inch; diameters of small cone, 1 inch and ¾ inch. No handle.

PROBLEM 37. To find the development of a cone truncated by an oblique plane. Axis of complete cone, 5 inches; axis of truncated part, 2½ inches; diameter of base, 3½ inches; slant of section, 30° to II.

27. Miscellaneous Problems Pertaining to Development.

A *double curved surface* is one that has no straight elements, like the surface of the *sphere*, the *torus*, the *ellipsoid*. etc. Such a surface can not be fully developed. All that can be done is to find a close approximation by dividing the surface by means of *meridians* into a number of *lunes* and arranging these on a plane. The larger the number of lunes is made, the less stretching or folding there will be. Tinners, who are often required to construct such forms out of tin, sheet iron, sheet zinc, or sheet copper, seldom use more than 12 lunes.

PROBLEM 38. To draw the covering for a sphere.

Draw the elevation or plan of the solid. Divide the circumference into 12 equal parts and lay these off on a straight line. With a radius of 9 of these parts draw a right and left arc through each division point, except the end points which require only one arc. These arcs will intersect above and below the straight line and form the required twelve lunes — an approximate covering for the sphere.

PROBLEM 39. To draw the covering for a sphere having a **diameter** of 4 inches. The covering to consist of four *zones* of equal width.

Tinners and coppersmiths sometimes construct globes of zones instead of *lunes*. When copper or some other highly malleable **metal can** be used, a little **hammering** of the four *conic surfaces*, which **form the** zones will **give the required** sphere.

DIVISION F.

THE HELIX.

28. General Principles of the Helix.

The curves may properly **be** divided into *plane curves*, such as the circle, the conic sections, the spiral, the trochoids, **etc.**, and into *space curves*, such as the *helix or screw line* which forms the subject of investigation of paragraphs 28, 29 and 30.

A *helix* is the locus of a point which moves along the surface **of a** cylinder in such a way that a constant ratio is maintained **between the** measure of its rotation and ascent.

FIG. 40.

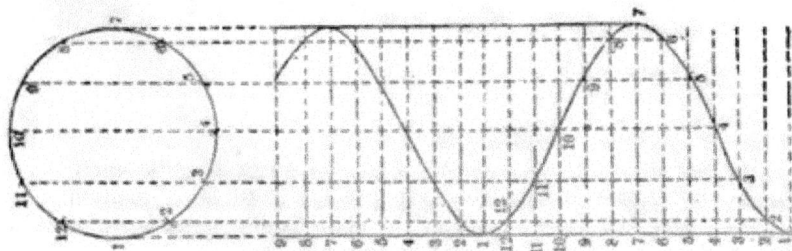

It is sometimes defined as a *spiral line* that constantly advances in the direction of a straight line called its axis. The student who has mastered the principles **of** Division E may assist his mind in imagining this line by developing the curved surface of a cylinder, drawing a diagonal or any oblique line in the development, and winding this again upon the solid. After the rewinding the diagonal becomes a helix.

The helix is sometimes called *screwline*, because it is found in the thread of every screw. See figures 35, 36, 37, 38 and 39.

If the curve ascends and passes from left to right in front of the axis, when the axis is vertical, the helix is said to be *right-hand*, and if it passes from right to left it is said to be *left hand*.

The *pitch* of a helix is the distance it advances along the axis in making one revolution.

FIGS. 35, 36, 37, 38, 39.

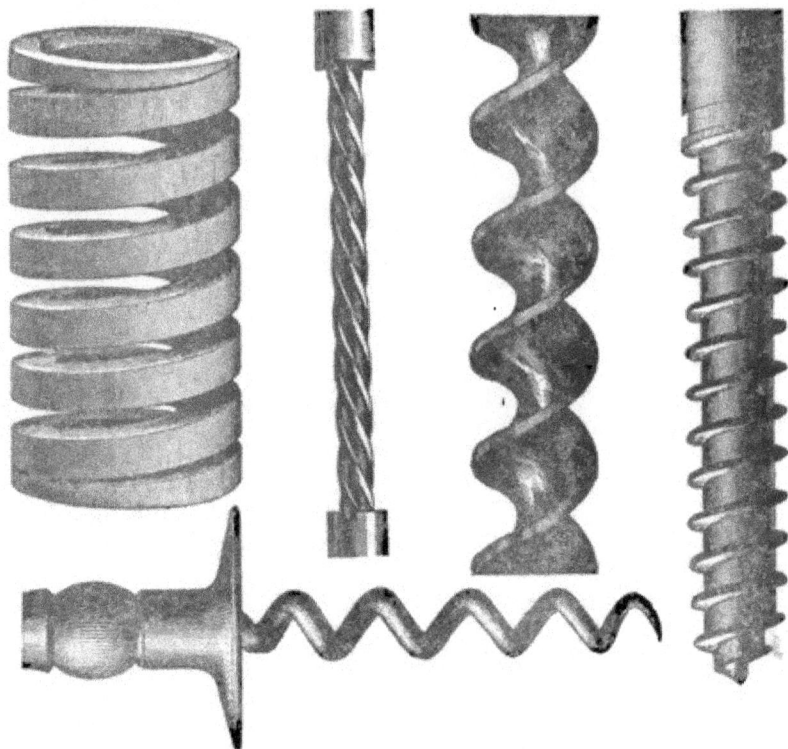

Solve the following problems:

PROBLEM 40. (FIG. 37). To draw the projections of a right-hand helical line 2 inches in diameter, 5 inches long, and 3 inches pitch.

PROBLEM 41. To draw a left-hand helix having the same dimensions and pitch as that of the last problem.

Careful study of figure 40. which is drawn ½ the required scale, will reveal the method of construction. The helix is drawn free-hand, through the located points.

29. The Helical Band, the Helical Flange, the Helicoid.

All surfaces may be divided into:

(1.) Planes,

(2.) Single curved surfaces (cylinder, cones),

(3.) Double curved surfaces (sphere, torus, ellipsoid),

(4.) Warped surfaces (helical flange, helicoid),

(5.) Irregular surfaces.

One of the surfaces **named** in the headline of the this paragraph belongs to the **second, and** two belong to **the** fourth class.

A *helical band* **is the** surface of a cylinder between equal and parallel helices. **See figures 35,** 38 and **42**

A *helical flange* is a warped surface that is **between two parallel** but unequal **helices** and is perpendicular to their **common axis. See figure** 41.

FIG. 41.

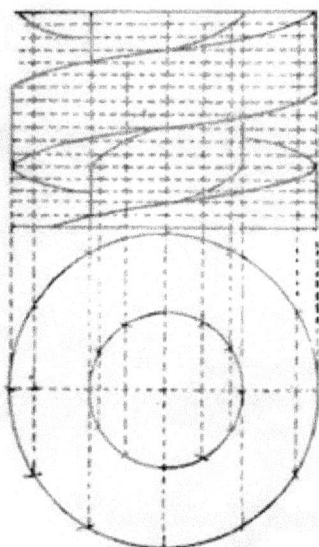

A *helicoid* is a warped surface that **is between two** parallel but unequal helices and is at an invariable acute angle to their axis. See figure 42.

It **may** be said that, as the circle and the straight line are the limiting **forms of** the ellipse, the helical flange is a limiting form of the **helicoid.**

A *serpentine* is a bent cylinder the axis of which is a helix. It is sometimes defined as the locus of a sphere, the center of which moves along a helix. **The** bed-spring and the cork screw furnish illustrations of this highly interesting space form. The groove of figure 37 is **a** *semi serpentine*. So is the groove of the drill described in problem 47

Solve the following problems:

PROBLEM 42.   To find the projections of a right-hand helical band, ¼ inch wide.   Diameter of cylinder, 3 inches; pitch, 1½ inch.

PROBLEM 43   To draw the projections of a left-hand helical flange ⅛ inch wide, 2 inches in outer diameter, 4 inches long, and 1½ inch pitch.

PROBLEM 44.   To draw the projections of a left-hand helicoid screw. Diameter of outer helix, 3 inches; diameter of inner helix, 2 inches; pitch, 1 inch.   Compare with figure 42.

PROBLEM 45.   To draw a right-hand flange screw of two threads (jack screw).   Diameter of the four outer helices, 4 inches; diameter of the four inner helices, 3 inches; pitch of each thread. 2 inches.   Compare figure 41.

FIG. 42.

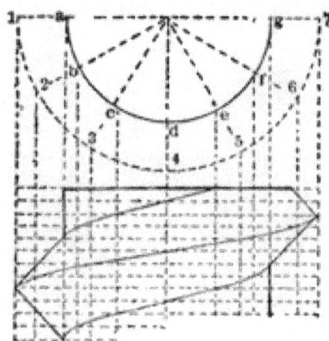

30.   Additional Problems on the Helix.

PROBLEM 46   To find the approximate projections of a three-inch rope consisting of 3 equal strands.   Pitch, 6 inches.

PROBLEM 47.   To find the approximate projections of a drill with a conical point.

A *drill* is simply a steel cylinder with a dull conical point, and a slightly enlarged square rear end for fastening it in the *brace*.   It has one *helical groove* of two revolutions and about 2¾ inches pitch.   The groove extends from the square rear end to the conical point and is semicylindric at every point.   Compare figure 37.

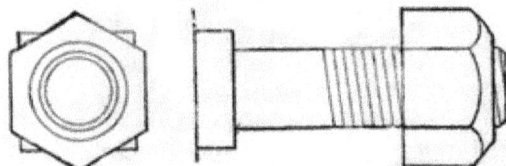

PROBLEM 48.   To find the projections of a helical stairway winding

about a column of 2 feet in diameter. Distance from floor to floor 10 feet, 8 inches; height of *riser*, 8 inches; diameter of whole *stairwell*, 18 feet. *Handrails, nosing* and *nosing moulds* not required.

PROBLEM 49. To draw a helix upon a cone.

With the exception of this problem the subject of conic helices has been omitted here as being beyond the reach of elementary graphics.

DIVISION G.

AXONOMETRIC PROJECTION.

31. General Principles of Axonometric Projection.

The three imaginary straight lines which represent the three dimensions, length, breadth and height of an object are called the *axes of dimension*. All trained geometricians imagine these axes as intersecting each other at right angles at the center of the solid, object or bulk to be measured.

In *axonometric projection* the object is drawn so that two or all axes of dimension form equal angles with the vertical plane of projection, while the horizontal plane of projection is dispensed with entirely.

When a solid or object is posed so that two of its axes of dimension are parallell to V and the third perpendicular to V, it is said to be in a *monodimetric position*, and when it is placed so that all three axes form equal angles with V, it is said to be in an *isometric position*. There are, therefore, two systems or methods of axonometric projection:

(1.) Monodimetric projection.

(2.) Isometric projection.

32. Monodimetric Projection.

In *monodimetric projection* the object is placed so that its principle and most characteristic *face* is parallel to the plane of projection, and can be drawn as it is. All other lines that are parallel to the principal face lines are also projected at their real lengths and in their real positions, while the lines that form right angles with the face, i. e. the lines parallel with the third axis of dimension. are drawn at angles of 45° to the horizontal and vertical lines of the front face either to right or left, up or down. *The length of such a retreating line is made equal to the shortest side of a triangle having angles of 105°, 45° 30°, and whose longest side equals the line to be represented.* A few worked problems will explain this somewhat complex statement.

PROBLEM 50. (Fig. 43). To draw the monodimetric projection of a cube of given dimension.

Draw A B equal to the given edge. Draw the square A B E D. Draw C A at 30° to A B, and B C at 45° to A B. The angle at C will evidently measure 105° Draw the remaining edges, representing those not visible by dotted lines.

FIG. 43.

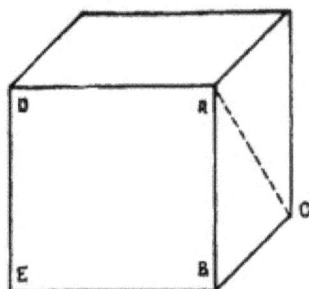

FIG. 44.

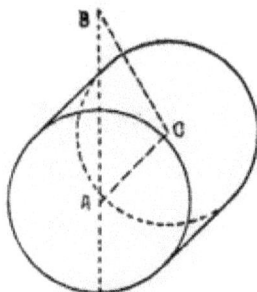

PROBLEM 51. (Fig. 44). To draw the monodimetric of a horizontal cylinder.

Locate A and draw, full size. the face circle. Draw A B equal to the length of the required axis. Draw C B at 30° and A C at 45° to A B. With C as the center draw the rear circle. Add the outline elements.

Solve the following problems.

PROBLEM 52. To construct the monodimetric of a horizontal hexagonal prism having a base side of 1¼ inch and an axis of 3¼ inches.

It is evident that this solid could be drawn in four different positions. Its lateral edges could be drawn so as to retreat to right and upward, to right and downward, to left and upward, to the left and downward. Select any of the three latter positions.

PROBLEM 53. To draw the monodimetric of a grindstone; radius, 2½ inches; thickness, ¼ inch; diameter of square hole at the center, ¼. inch.

No conditions as to position being given, it is evident that the grindstone may be drawn in any monometric position. What are these positions? Draw the object in one of the four positions stated above.

PROBLEM 54. To draw the monodimetric of a waterbucket having an axis of 1 foot, a base diameter of 10 inches, a top diameter of 14 inches, and a thickness in every part of 1 inch. Add two 1-inch hoops and a semicircular wire handle. Finish the drawing neatly.

33. Monodimetric Projection of Non-Axial Lines.

The following worked problem is intended to answer the question of how to represent and measure lines that are not parallel to axes of dimension.

PROBLEM 55. (**Fig.** 45). To find the monodimetric of a horizontal pentagon.

Draw a diagram of the figure (Fig. 32 or 36, **Vol. I**) and in it draw the lines 5 6 and 3 4. Draw A B equal to 1 2. Draw 7 D at 45° to A B, and make it equal to 5 6 by ⅓3. Find point F in the same names. Make F E and F C equal to the halves of 34. Draw the outline.

By drawing five **equal** vertical lines at the angular **points of the** monodimetric pentagon, **and by** connecting the upper ends **of these verti-** cals, the monodimetric **of a** pentagonal prism is obtained.

Still another monodimetric projection may be obtained by drawing the lateral edges of the prism downward, making the number of possible cases not four, but six.

FIG. 45.

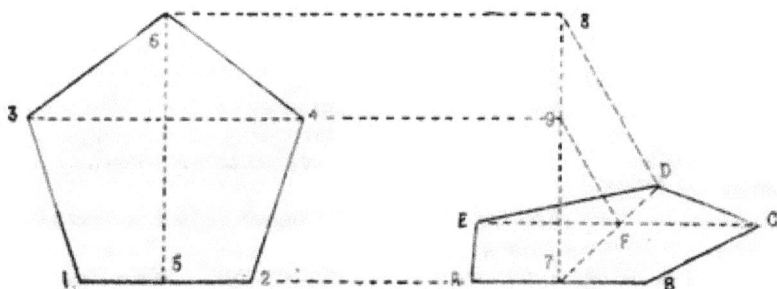

Solve the following problems:

PROBLEM 56. To find the monodimetric of a vertical heptagonal pyramid.

PROBLEM 57. To find the monodimetric of a truncated triangular pyramid. **Height of** *frustrum*. 3 inches; side of base, **3 inches**; side of section, 2 inches

It is difficult to **find the** monodimetric of a horizontal circle. When a circular object **is to be drawn**, it should be posed so that **the circles will** be parallel to V.

34. Additional Problems in Monodimetric Projection.

Monodimetric projection is much used in drawing *details* of stone and lumber construction, such as *mortise-joints*, *dovetail-joints*, *miter-joints*, *stretcher-joints*, building hardware, brick and stone arches, etc It is therfore often called *shop perspective*, *false perspective*, *parallel perspect-ive*, or *cabinet perspective*. In as much as a monodimetric projection shows the front and two sides of the object, it resembles a true perspective pict-ure; but it is not drawn in accordance with the laws of linear perspective, and these terms are entirely improper and confusing. The student should not use them.

Solve the following problems:

PROBLEM 58. To draw the monodimetric of a table, foot-stool, or tool bench.

PROBLEM 59. To draw the monodimetric of any three of the Egyptian letters of ¶ 47, enlarging them to four diameters and giving them a thickness of ½ inch.

PROBLEM 60. To draw the monodimetric of a dovetailed box with a half-open sliding lid. Add the scale.

PROBLEM 61. To draw the monodimetric of a saw-horse. Add the scale.

These figures are to be drawn on a large scale so that each will fill a page. The rear edges are to be shown in dotted lines. The edges which divide front faces from side faces are to be drawn in bold black lines, and all other visible edges are to be made in light black lines.

35. General Principles of Isometric Projection.

The difference of *monodimetric* and *isometric* projection has already been stated in paragraph 31. It is this:

In monodimetric projection the object is *posed* so that two of its axes of dimension are parallel, and the third axis perpendicular, to V, while in isometric projection the object is represented so that all three axes form equal angles with V.

An *isometric drawing* of an object is, therefore, a real projection, while a monodimetric drawing is not.

Careful study of the following isometric projections of a cube and an oblong frame will make clear these statements.

FIG. 46   FIG. 47.

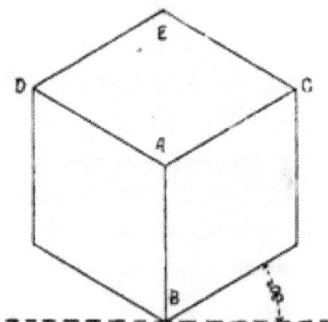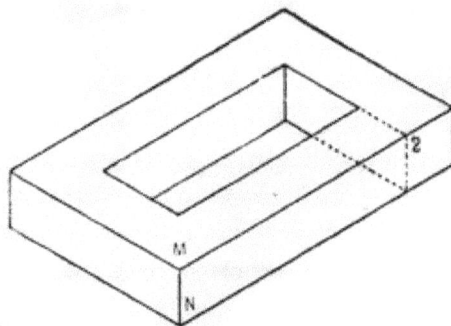

Every edge of these solids is parallel to one of the three axes of dimension and all form equal angles with V. It follows that all are shortened equally, i. e., according to the same ratio. They bear the same relation to each other in the projection as they do in reality.

Having fully mastered this principle, the student should now try to understand that, if the projection of an object is enlarged so as to make every axis of dimension, and every line parallel to an axis of dimension, equal to the real axis or line, no scale will be needed at all, i. e., that:

In an isometric projection every *axial line* (line parallel to an axis of dimension) is directly measurable.

This principle, introduced by Prof. Moellinger, a noted Swiss mathematician, is the one which has made isometric projection valuable, because in almost every object of industrial art the axial lines abound.

With regard to position, it may be said.that in an isometric projection

(1.) The vertical lines remain vertical.

(2.) The horizontal *axial* lines form angles of 30°, to right or left, with G L.

(3.) The length and position of *non-axial* lines may be found by making them *face diagonals* or *space diagonals* in rectangular blocks formed by axial lines.

PROBLEM 62. To draw the isometric of a square box, open at the top. Dimensions, 4 by 3 by 2 inches; thickness of boards, ¼ inch. Show its construction and the nail heads.

36. The Circle in Isometric.

The circle may be drawn in isometric by inclosing it in a square, drawing this in isometric, and inscribing an ellipse.

FIG. 48.　　　　　　　　FIG. 49.

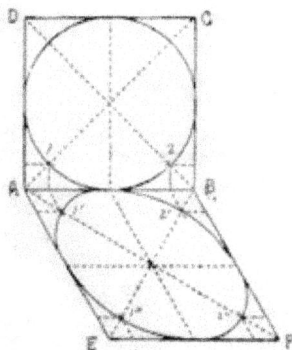 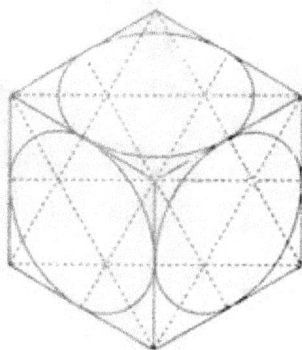

Thus, let A B C D (Fig. 48) be a square inclosing a circle, to be drawn in isometric. The square will appear as a rhombus A B F E, having angles of 60° and 120°. Draw the diameters of the square and draw lines representing these in the rhombus. Draw the diagonals in the square and rhombus. Find the points where the ellipse crosses the rhombus diagonals. The illustration shows how these points may be found. Draw the ellipse freehand.

Fortunately, this special form of the ellipse can be easily imitated with the compasses (oval). An examination of figure 49, representing a cube with circles inscribed within each visible face, will explain the *modus operandi* of this convenient approximation.

Solve the following problems:

PROBLEM 63. To draw the isometric of a vertical cylinder. Axis, 3¼ inches; diameter, 2½ inches.

PROBLEM 64. To draw the isometric of a horizontal cylinder having the same dimensions.

37. Isometric Projection of Non-Isometric Lines.

The following worked problem illustrates how non-isometric lines or figures are drawn in isometric, and how the real length of non-isometric lines may be found by construction.

PROBLEM 65. (Figs. 50 and 51). To make an isometric drawing of an hexagonal prism.

Draw a diagram of the base of the prism inclosed by a rectangle, A B C D. Draw this rectangle in isometric where it will form a rhomboid with angles of 60° and 120°. Make E′ 1′ equal to A 1, 2′ F′ equal to 2 B, E′ 6′ equal to A 6, etc. This will give the isometric of the regular hexagon. Then draw the vertical edges equal to the real height of the prism. Lastly connect the upper ends of the verticals by lines forming the upper isometric hexagon.

FIG 50. 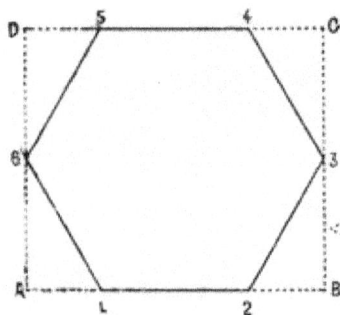   FIG. 51.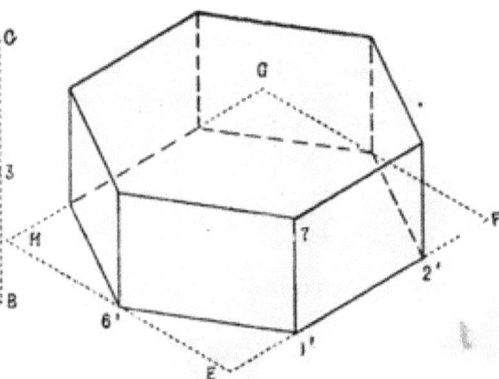

In this way all non-isometrical figures are drawn They are first inscribed within some figure that can be drawn in isometric.

Solve the following problems:

PROBLEM 67. To find the isometric of a pentagonal prism. Horizontal edge, 1½ inch; vertical edge, 3 inches.

PROBLEM 68. To draw the isometric of an irregular heptagonal pyramid, from given orthographic projections.

PROBLEM 69. To draw the isometric of a carpenter's trestle.

PROBLEM 70. To draw the isometric of a tool bench with braces for stiffening its legs.

38. **Cone and** Sphere in Isometric.

PROBLEM 71. (Fig. 52). To draw **a cone in isometric. Diameter,** 3½ inches; axis, 4 inches.

PROBLEM 72. (Fig. 53) To make an isometric drawing of **a hemi-**sphere having a radius of 2 inches.

Find the isometric of the great circle, as in the former problem. Then draw a semicircle over the major axis of the ellipse. Remember that a sphere projects as a circle, no matter how it may be posed.

Fig. 52.   Fig. 53.

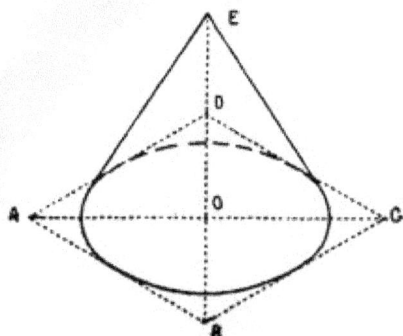

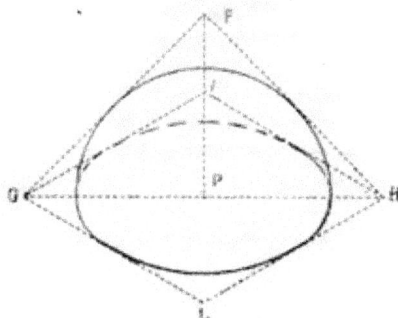

PROBLEM 73 To find the real **radius of a given isometric** sphere.

This problem is more difficult **than might appear at first.** Remember that only axial lines can be measured. Such a line might be drawn through the center, but it would evidently not terminate in the outline (principal meridian) of the sphere Any diameter in the circle representing the sphere would be too long. In isometric all figures are drawn larger than in orthographic in order that their axial lines may appear as they are. How will you go to work to find it?

Let this problem be a test for you.

DIVISION H.

SHADOWS.

39. **The Light Parallel to V.**

The form of the *shadow* of an object depends on:

(1.) The object casting the shadow, i. e., the outline which the object presents to the light.

(2.) The surface upon which the shadow falls.

(3.) The source or direction of the light.

In mechanical drawing the *rays of light* are supposed to have some *fixed direction*, and in all examples and problems of this division the rays of light are assumed to be parallel, so that the direction of one ray is the direction of all.

The simplest conditions prevail when the light is parallel to V and falls upon II at an angle of 45°. The horizontal projections of the rays can then be drawn with the T-square and the vertical projections with the right-angled isosceles triangle. All shadows will be on the right side of the object and appear in II, the shadow of a point being where a ray of light through the point would pierce the surface upon which the shadow is cast.

The solution of problems under these stated conditions is so simple that a study of figures 54 and 55 should be sufficient for the successful working by the student of all such problems.

FIG. 54   FIG. 55.

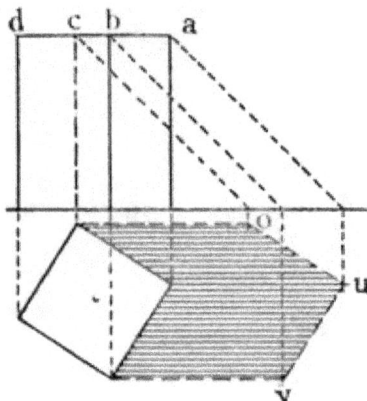
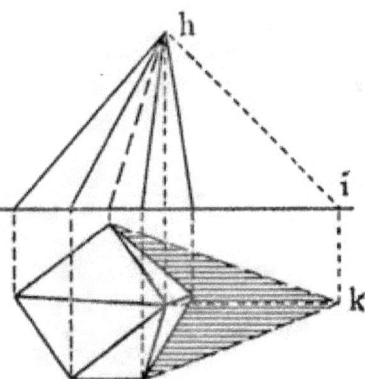

Figure 54 solves the problem, to find the shadow of a rectangular block; and figure 55, to find the shadow of an irregular pentagonal pyramid.

Solve the following problems for which no figures or solutions are given:

PROBLEM 74. To find the shadow of an irregular, obliquely truncated pentagonal prism.

PROBLEM 75. To find the shadow of a right cylinder.

This problem can be solved by finding the shadow of a series of points in the upper circle and by connecting these by a freehand stroke with the shadow of the elments tangent to the light. A better way, however, is to find the shadow of the upper base, remembering that the shadow of any plane form cast upon a parallel plane must be equal to the form, etc.

PROBLEM 76. To find the shadow of a cylinder **resting upon H and having its axis** perpendicular to V

PROBLEM 77. To find the shadow of **a truncated oblique cone.**

40. The Light Oblique to H and V.

The next step is to assume **the rays of light** oblique to **both planes of** projection. The simplest conditions of this kind prevail when the descending rays are **assumed so as to give** horizontal and **vertical projec-** tions of 45° to G L. **The student will observe** that in this case **the** *real angle of inclination* and *declination* is not 45°, **but that it is less. It is** equal to the angle which the *space diagonal* of a cube form with the base of the cube, i. e., **an angle of** about 37½°.

The shadow is cast to **the right and rear of the** object and if this should **stand close to V, a** part of the shadow will fall **upon V. Figure** 56 represents a triangle in space placed obliquely **to V and H. The** shadow falls **upon both** planes of projection and forms a dihedral, **which gives a pentagonal development.** The direction which the shadow **of AB and BC takes in crossing** G L is found by obtaining the shadow of inter- mediate points. **Figure 57 shows how to find the shadow of a square prism placed so that none of its lateral faces is parallel to V, and that the shadow will fall upon H and V.**

FIG. 56.   FIG. 57.

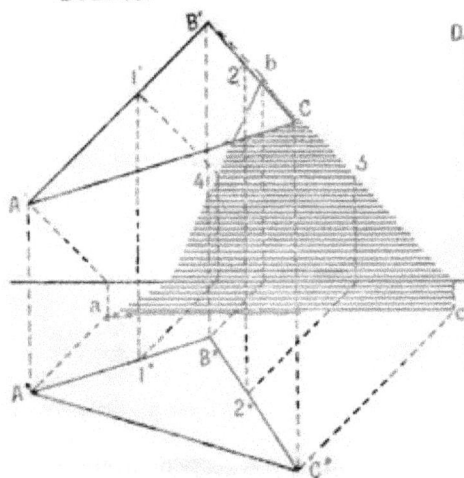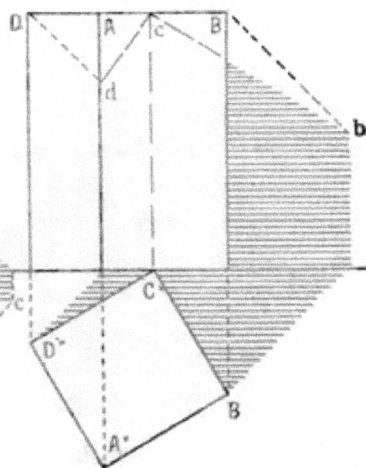

The student who is able to read every line of these two figures should have no great difficulty in solving the following problems. Let him remember the following:

(1.) The shadow of a vertical line forms an angle of 45° with G L, upon H, **and** is perpendicular to G L, upon V.

(2.) **The** shadow of a line perpendicular to V forms an angle of 45° with G L, upon V, and is perpendicular to G L, upon H.

(3.) The shadow of a line parallel to V is equal and parallel to the line, upon V.

(4.) The shadow of a line parallel to II is equal and parallel to the line, upon H.

Solve the following problems:

PROBLEM 78. To find the shadow cast upon II of a cube.

PROBLEM 79. To find the shadow cast upon II and V of a tall, irregular pentagonal prism.

PROBLEM 80. To find the shadow cast upon II and V of a hexagonal pyramid standing upon its apex.

PROBLEM 81. To find the shadow of an irregular pentagonal pyramid having its axis parallel to V and H.

41.   Shadows of Circles and Curved Surfaces.

In problems 75, 76 and 77 the student has already solved problems pertaining the shadows of objects having curved surfaces. In the following problems the direction of the light rays is the same as in paragraph 40.

FIG. 58.

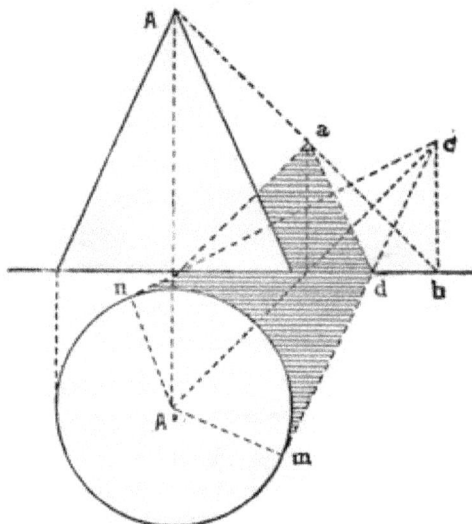

PROBLEM 82. To find the shadow upon II of a vertical circle whose plane is parallel to V.

PROBLEM 83. To find the shadow upon H and V of a horizontal circle.

PROBLEE 84. To find the shadows in II and V of a circle whose plane is perpendicular to G L.

PROBLEM 85. To find the shadow in II and V of a vertical cone.

The method of solution (Fig. 58) is somewhat peculiar. Find the shadow of the apex upon V, then imagine V as *transparent* and find where the shadow of the apex would fall if such were the case. It would evidently be cast upon the extended or rear part of H, directly behind B, i. e., at C. Draw tangents from C to the base circle, and you will obtain the shadow of the cone upon H and its rear extension. Consider now V as opaque and find the shadow upon it.

PROBLEM 86. To find the shadow of a cone standing upon its apex near V.

42. The Shadow of the Sphere.

PROBLEM 87. (Fig. 59.) To find the shadow in II of a sphere.

FIG. 59.

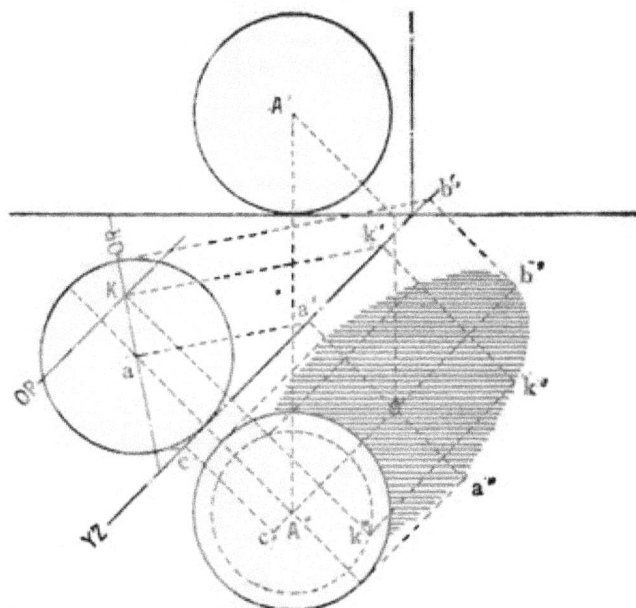

The shadow of a sphere is equal to the shadow of the one of its *great circles* which is *perpendicular to the rays of light*. If this great circle is found, the remaining part of the problem can present but few difficulties. The work may be done as follows:

(1.) Find the shadow of the center of the sphere.

(2) Locate an auxiliary plane perpendicular to II and parallel to the descending rays of light.

(3.) Upon this plane draw an auxiliary vertical projection of the sphere.

(4.) Draw QṘ, the great circle, at right angles to the rays of light. This is done by finding the obstructed ray of light through the center A from its horizontal projection, and by drawing Q R perpendicular to it.

(5) Draw tangent rays at Q R, parallel to a a'. These will give

the major diameter of the ellipse which will form the shadow.   The minor diameter will be equal to the diameter of the sphere.

(6.) Draw the ellipse by one of the methods given in paragraph 18, or find additional points by the method shown in figure 59, i. e., by using planes parallel to II, like O P.

PROBLEM 88.   To find the shadow of a sphere, cast upon V.

In monodimetric and isometric projection shades are often, but shadows rarely, required. The rays of light are usually assumed so that the shadow of every perpendicular line becomes a horizontal line equal in length to the perpendicular, i. e., the rays are assumed to come from the left, the front and above. In this case every obstructed ray can be drawn with the right angled isosceles triangle placed against the T-square. The shadows that are not cast upon parts of this object are assumed to fall upon an imaginary horizontal plane supporting the object.

All shadows given in this book are assumed to be produced by straight or circular outlines and to be cast upon II or V. Book III, Descriptive Geometry, continues the subject and shows how to find shadows cast upon oblique and single curved surfaces by objects having more complex outlines.

PART II.

Shading and Draughting.

43. The Object.

The object of this course in *shading* and *draughting* is to teach the student the methods of representing complex objects; to familiarize him with the use of the scale and the common measuring tools, and to develop his taste with regard to the disposition of details, inscriptions, etc. It is intended that this work should be carried on simultaneously with the work of Part I, i. e., that every alternate lesson should be given to *draughting in the class-room* under the supervision of the teacher. While all work in graphics must be done carefully and neatly, this work, requiring larger sheets of paper and involving more complex subjects, will be especially suited for the training of the æsthetic qualities of the student—an educational end never to be neglected, though difficult of attainment.

44. Tools and Materials.

In addition to the tools required for the home work and described in Part I, each student must be provided with the following:

Fig. 60

(1.) *A drawing-board.* The board needed in this work should measure 14 to 18 inches by 22 to 24 inches, and should be made of good quality of well-seasoned white pine lumber, glued together of about four strips. One or both of the short ends should be provided with a crosspiece (header) of soft maple, cherry or some other small-grained wood. The header must, of course, be *straight*. Fig. 1 represents such a board with two headers, and the above illustration shows how a larger and better, though more expensive, board may be made.

(2.) *A T-square*, with blade extending across the board. The simple construction shown in Fig. 62 makes this form preferable to any other for the beginner.

FIG. 61.

(3.) *Two triangles*, 60°, 30°, 90°, and 45°, 90°, respectively. The sides of these should measure not less than 6 inches. Good work may be done with the right-angled isosceles triangle alone. Many practical draughtsmen use the *tetrangle* shown in Fig. 63, in preference to two triangles.

FIG. 62.

(4.) *Four white metal thumb tacks* to fasten the sheet to the drawing-board.

FIG. 63.

(5.) *A paper measure*, i. e., a strip of tough, smooth paper, 1¼ by 16 inches, printed with lines showing inches and halves, quarters, eighths and sixteenths of inches. Paper measures are better than any other cheap measuring tools, and cost but few cents per piece.

45. General Remarks.

In school where a considerable number of drawing-boards are used, it will be cheaper to have them made to order in some carpenter shop. The other tools, however, should be bought of the instrument dealer. The cheaper grade of T-squares and triangles are usually made of beech or pear wood; the best are the transparent celluloid tools called *amber*.

For storing the drawing-boards between lessons, the class-room or an adjoining closet-room ought to be provided with a *drawing-board rack*, i. e., a strong square case, open on one side, into which the boards may be slit separately between cleats. The boards should lie horizontally with the drawing sheet on the under side; the upper side will then serve as a shelf for the deposition of the paper measure and the triangle The top of the case should be of strong pine lumber, so that it may be used as a table for paper cutting and the deposition of ink saucers. models. etc.

Wherever the conditions make it possible, it is well to provide *the drawing room* with top-light, and to furnish it with drawing tables that can be used either sitting or standing. There are a number of such tables in the market. The best, though not the cheapest, school drawing table known to the author of this book is the Eugene Dietzgen patent drawing table I. X. L.

46. Use of Instruments and Materials.

The T-square is used to draw parallel lines by sliding its head along the left side of the drawing-board and using the upper edge of the blade as a straight edge. It should never be used on another side as the edges of the board are seldom exactly parallel or at right-angles with each other. Before ruling the line, the blade should be pressed firmly on the paper, as the square is liable to move slight'y. unless the head of the square and the board exactly coincide. The square should be moved along the side of the board by the left hand. leaving the right hand free for the use of the pencil or the pen.

Triangles are used as straight edges for drawing perpendicular and oblique lines to those already drawn by the T-square. They are used also for drawing parallel lines, by placing the edge of one along the line to which the parallel is to be drawn, and by sliding the other triangle.

Ink.—In practical draughting India ink is used, instead of writing ink. The India-ink is preferable in that it can stand moisture without spreading. It is also blacker and covers the paper better, though it is more expensive. especially when bought in liquid form. Many designers buy India-ink sticks and prepare each day as much as they expect to use. Fig. 64 represents a stick of dry India-ink.

FIG. 64.

To prepare the India-Ink.—Rub a stick of the ink on a saucer or ink-slab containing about a teaspoonful of water until the proper consistency is obtained. To determine the latter, try the ink from time to time with a drawing-pen on a piece of paper, and if, when *dry.* a perfectly black (not gray) line is left, the ink is ready for use. When ground it should always be kept covered over, to prevent its drying quickly, and so becoming thick. The end of the stick of ink should be wiped after rubbing, as otherwise it is liable to crumble It is also a good plan, when a long stick is used, to wrap tin-foil tightly around it, to prevent its thus breaking or cracking.

Mounting the Paper —Lay the paper upon the drawing-board smooth side up. Insert one of the thumb tacks close to the edge in a corner of the sheet. Square the sheet with the board by means of the T-square. Insert the other thumb tacks.

The Pencil Sketch —All drawings should be made in pencil before inking. The penciled lines should be made fine and light with a hard pencil, so as to be easily erased or inked over. To erase strong pencil marks requires hard rubbing, which destroys the surface of the paper. All penciling should be done carefully to avoid confusion in inking.

The tint lines and shade lines are usually drawn in ink without any sketching.

Inking.—Fill the drawing pen by means of a writing pen and keep the outside of the blades clean Hold it nearly upright and carry it along the blade of the T-square from left to right, with the flat sides parallel to the direction of the line. Use only the upper edge of the T-square. Carefully clean the pen when through using In inking the horizontal lines should be first drawn, commencing at the top, and then the vertical lines commencing at the left. This will reduce the liability to blot the work before it is dry. Never use the blotting paper.

47. Inscriptions.

It is important that the student of projection drawing should learn to write and draw neat inscriptions. Well-made inscriptions greatly enhance the beauty of a drawing. They serve as an indication of equal care taken in the execution of the construction. For this reason the plate of the so-called *Egyptian* capitals and numbers, printed in Vol I, is here reprinted, not to be copied, but for reference. There is also added a complete alphabet of capitals, small letters, and numbers of *round writing*, a style of letters so-called because of its predominant round form. On account of its distinctness, beauty, and ease of construction, no other style can surpass it for inscription purposes.

The letters and figures of this style should not be drawn, but written. After some practice the writing may be done with almost any large and elastic pen. It is best, however to procure a pen made specially for the purpose, such as F. Soennecker's No. 2 or 3. Larger letters are made with a good shading pen, or F. Soennecker's Parcel's pen No. 133. Students who wish to practice round writing would do well to procure F. Soennecker's Text Book of Round Writing, published by the Keuffel Esser Co., New York, 127 Fulton Street.

THE EGYPTIAN.

A B C D E F G H I J K L M N

O P Q R S T U V W X Y Z

1 2 3 4 5 6 7 8 9 0 .

A B C D E F G H I K
L M N O P Q R S
T U V W X Y Z

a b c d e f g ff ffi ffl fi fj fk fl ll m n o p q r
s t u v w x y z

1 2 3 4 5 6 7 8 9 0

For many purposes a written plain vertical letter will answer best.

48. Blue-printing and Black-printing.

The invention of the beautiful processes of *blue* or *black-printing* and *photo zinc etching* has, of late, greatly changed the methods of work in practical draughting. Formerly most drawings were finished in colors applied with the brush, but at present nearly all ordinary work is being done in black lines.

In order to reproduce a drawing by the blue or black-printing process, it is first made in pencil the same as every other drawing. It is then traced in strong India-ink upon a sheet of transparent paper called *tracing paper* or *patera*.

The next step is to coat the *blue-print paper* with sensitive material. The paper is simply common drawing or writing paper, usually *French satin*. The material is a mixture in nearly equal parts of dissolved *cit. iron and ammonium* and *pot. perrocyanide*. These chemicals are dissolved separately in clean water, in a ratio of about two tablespoons of each compound, finely ground, to one cup of water, and allowed to stand in bottles in a dark place for about forty-eight hours. The paper is then tacked to a wall in an entirely dark room, the two solutions are poured into a cup, and the mixture is carefully applied to the paper with a large, smooth paint-brush or a sponge. It dries rapidly and will be ready for use in two to three hours.

The printing is done as follows: The sheet of sensitized paper is laid, coated side up, upon a drawing-board; the tracing is laid over it; a plate of thick glass is laid over the latter to hold it down at every point, and the whole is exposed to the bright sunlight for about five minutes, when the whole surface of the coated sheet will have turned from a light yellow to a dirty bluish gray. It is then immediately immersed in a bath of clean water. The water will wash off the coating where it was not fixed by the sunlight, i. e , under the black lines of the tracing, and these will appear white, while the rest of the surface will turn a brilliant blue. It is evident that as many copies can be made of a tracing as may be desired. In architects' and engineers' draughting rooms more complex apparatus is used than the one here described, but the process is the same.

Formerly every artisan or artist prepared his own paper. For the last half-dozen years, however, factories of sensitized paper have been established in all large cities, and carefully prepared " blue paper " costs now but little more than other paper. The difficulty with " ready blue paper " is in that it must be kept in a dark place. An exposure to sunlight of only a few seconds will start the chemical action and render it valueless. All schools of applied mathematics have blue-printing rooms connected with their classrooms in draughting, and finish their work in white upon blue ground.

The *black-printing process* does not differ from the blue-printing process in the manipulation of the drawing. The lines appear black upon light gray or mottled ground. The paper is difficult to prepare and is, therefore, bought ready for printing The materials cost more than those used in blue-printing. As a result the process is used almost only by sculupturers and woodcarvers in whose drawings the blue-printing process would reverse light and shade.

Photo-zinc etching requires a considerable amount of costly apparatus, and the work of etching, though it is a purely chemical manipulation, requires a good deal of skill. It is, therefore, done only in special art establishments. The product, a relief plate, can be used in every printing press. Nearly all line pictures in the books and newspapers of to-day are printed from photo-zinc etchings made from pen drawings, and every well-made pen drawing may thus be photograved. All the illustrations of this book were printed from photo-zinc etching made from pen drawings most of which were prepared by L. P. Brous. student assistant in the Department of Industrial Art at the Kansas State Agricultural College.

49. Shades.

Plate I. This figure represents the vertical and horizontal projections of a *group of solids* consisting of a square slab, broken off behind, an octagonal prism, a cylinder and an octagonal pyramid.

The group is placed so that the *source of light* is to the front, the left and above. and the shadow to the rear and right. Some of the faces of the group, especially of the pyramid, are nearly at right angles to the light rays, and receive evidently more light, proportionately, than the horizontal surfaces, or some of the faces of the prism and parts of the cylinder. Along two of the elements of the cylinder the light rays are tangent only, i. e , they merely graze the object The parts of the solids on the opposite or rear side of the group receive only reflected, but no direct, light. It is these different light effects, which may be watched on every object, that the shaded drawing represents.

In order to shade an object properly, the student must be able to estimate approximately the quantity of light received by every part of the surface, or, which is the same, the angle which every part of the surface forms with the light rays.

There are, however, a few exceptions or modifications to this rule. In the first place, there is the influence of the distance of the object from the eye. Things near the eye display more contrasts of light and shade than things farther away. while at any great distance all shades and lights, and even colors, seem to blend into one general tone. This is due to the fact that objects appear smaller at a distance, and that the atmosphere is slightly opaque. It may be said then. that *dark surfaces grow lighter and light surfaces darker as they recede*. In projection drawing it is necessary to greatly exaggerate the difference of shade between the nearer and farther parts of a surface in order to show the difference of distance from the eye.

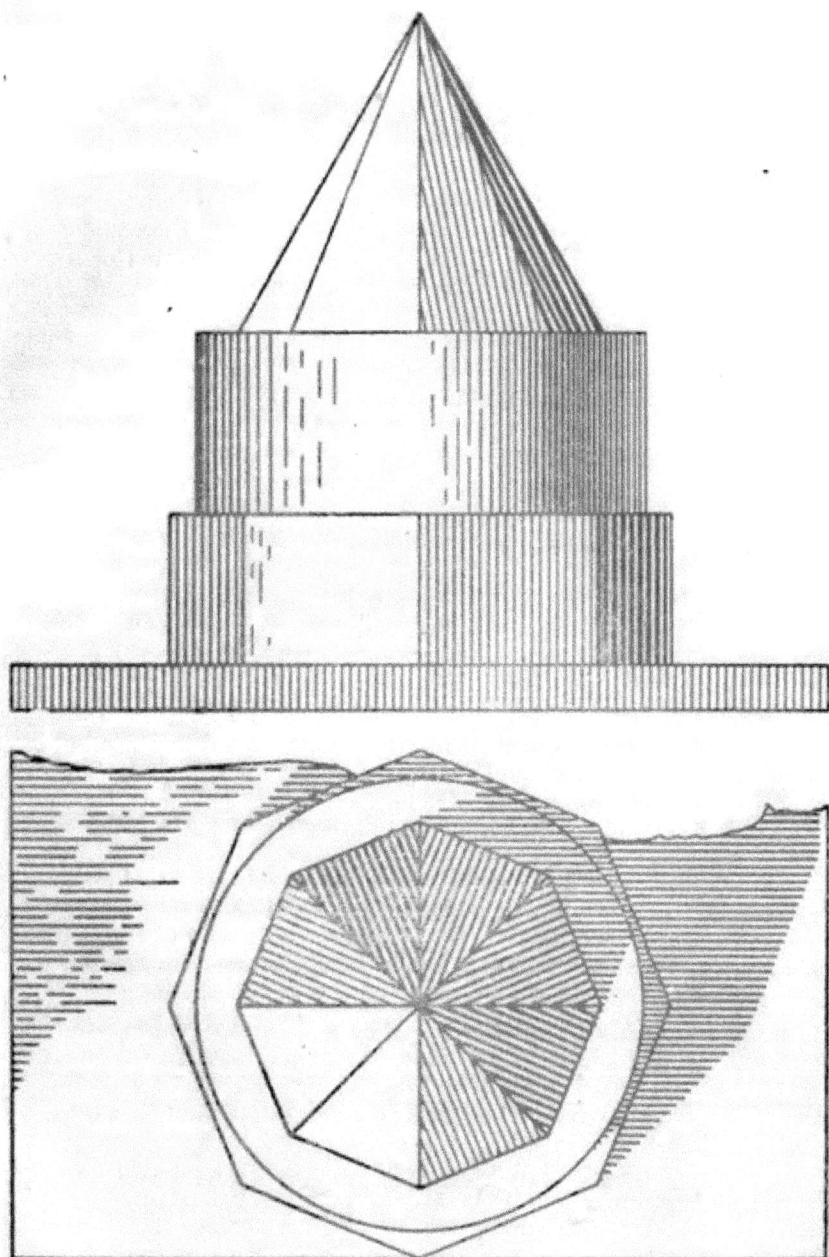

In the second place, there is the influence of contrast. The light parts appear lighter near dark parts, and the dark parts seem darker close to light parts. This fact is well-known by every one and is taken advantage of in decorating and drawing. As a consequence the shading of the group of solids is strongest where the shaded surfaces are adjacent to light surfaces, and vice versa.

Upon objects having curved surfaces like the cylinder, the depth of shade must change at every element. The brightest part is a little forward of the point in H where the horizontal projection of a ray of light through the axis of the cylinder would pierce the circle which forms the horizontal projection of the cylinder. This part of the curved surface is called *the brilliant line*. It is placed forward of the element which reclines the most to the light, because the light of this element, according to a well-known law in physics, would be reflected back from whence it came, while the light from elements a little more to the right would be reflected forward in the direction of the observer. The latter elements, though receiving less light, would really appear lighter.

The darkest parts of the surface are the elements nearest the point of tangency. The surface from to the outline at the right should apparently be of the same shade, being all in the shadow. But here another principle has to be observed. There is always a small amount of light coming in exactly the opposite direction from the orignal one. This is called reflected light, and, owing to this, the surface to the right is made a little lighter as it turns back. See figure 68.

This principle influences also the shading of the pyramid.

A careful study of the given group of solids will reveal a number of applications of the exceptions mentioned. The student should not draw a single line, the meaning of which he does not understand. In case he cannot find reasons for drawing certain lines, he should ask the eacher for an explanation.

The outlines of the shadows are found by drawing at 45° to G L, tangent to the outlines in II. The shadow of the pyramid is found by establishing the shadow of the apex upon the level of the base of the pyramid, and drawing from there, in II, tangent to the base of this solid.

The figure should be copied twice its linear dimensions, i. e., four times as large as the given original. The outline should be carefully laid out in pencil and inked. The shade lines should be drawn without any sketching and should be made as near as possible like the original in thickness—not stronger. The figure being larger, there should be an increased number of shade lines.

All *outlines* separating light from dark surfaces should be drawn considerably stronger than those separating faces of equal or nearly equal light effects. This rule should be followed in all mechanical drawing, and must not be neglected in drawing the problems of Part I, though nothing is said there about shading.

Provide the plate with a uniform border line.

In the upper left corner of the plate write a neat inscription in *round writing*, as described in paragraph 47.

In the lower right corner add your signature.

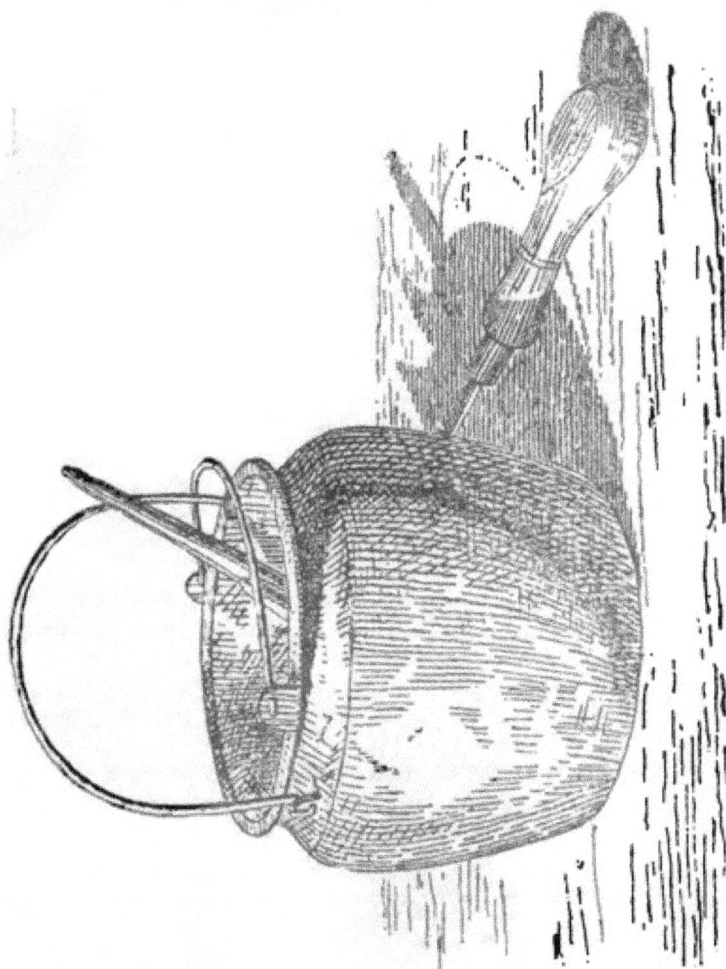

FIG. 68.

50. Shades upon Complex Surfaces.

PLATE II. This plate represents a group of solids consisting of three well-known geometric forms and a part of the shaft of a fluted column.

The direction of the light is the same as in the last plate, and there are no new principles involved. The solids, however, are more complex and require a more subtle grading of shade lines. The strongest shade lines of the fluted shaft and the cone are made by drawing two light

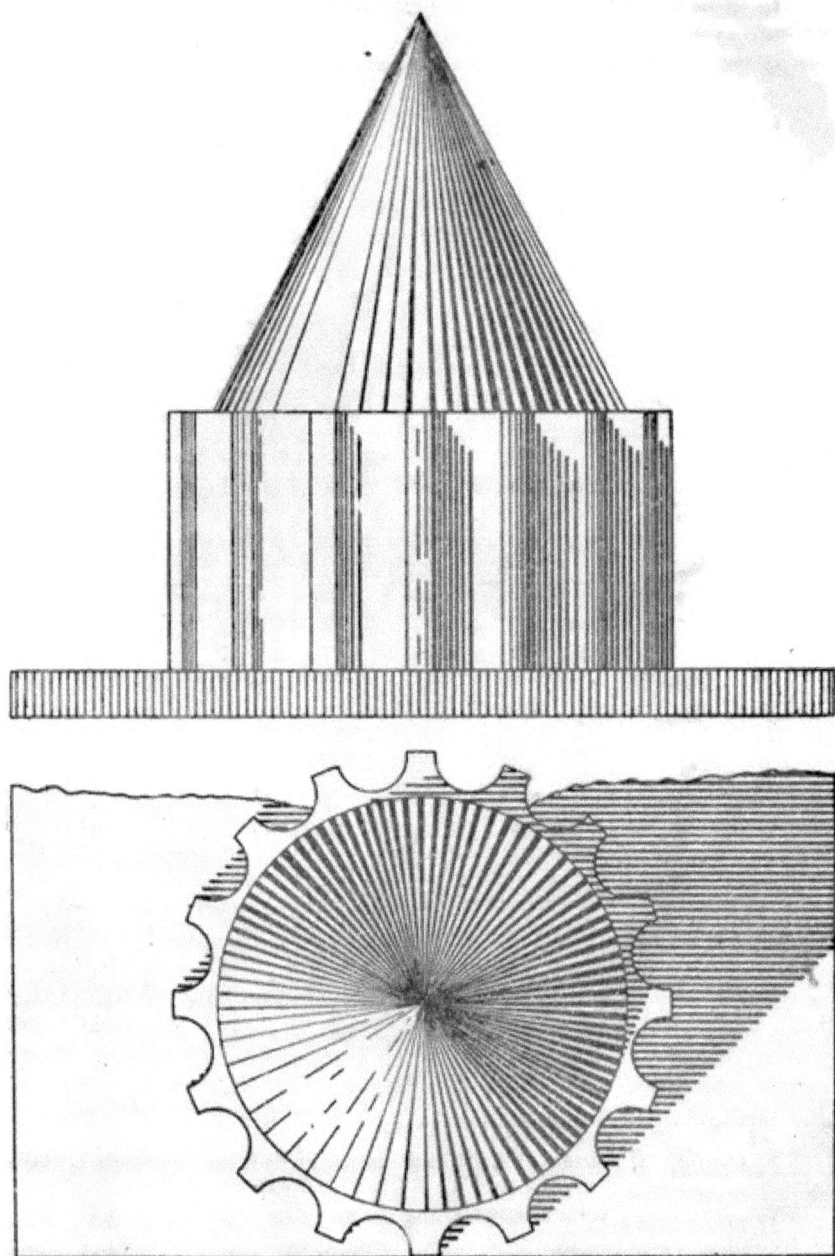

outlines for each and filling the space between the two by drawing an other line or two with the drawing pen. To shade such a plate well requires careful study of the principles involved and a close application in the work.

Draw the figure not less than two diameters of the original.

Add a neat border line.

In the upper left corner inside the border line write a neat inscription in *round writing*, as described in paragraph 47.

In the lower right corner sign your name.

51. Shades upon Double Curved Surfaces.

PLATE III shows a *cavetto*, a *sphere* and a *cone*, shaded by means of irregularly placed points or dots. Such shading or tinting is called *stippling*. It is done with the common writing pen, and is not difficult to learn. The principles of shading are, of course, the same, no matter what graphic method may be followed in producing the desired effect.

The student should take care not to place the dots in rows, but to distribute them evenly over the surface, much as the farmer sows the seed upon a field, i. e., irregular in position, but regular in distribution.

Note that the sphere has its *brilliant point* not where the light is perpendicular to the surface, but somewhat nearer the center of the projection. The reasons for this are those given with regard to the shading of the cylinder in plate I. The light rays are tangent to the sphere along a great circle which projects in II and V as an eIlipse. The rear surface of the sphere is somewhat lighter than the region where the light is tangent, for reasons already stated.

The shadows of the cone upon the sphere and the shadow of the sphere upon the scotia is not expected to be found by the pupil, but should be copied from the original plate. The proper solution of these two problems must be left to *higher descriptive geometry*. Remember that all shadows appear strongest along the outline and lighter toward the middle.

Fig. 68, which represents a carpenter's glue-pot with glue brushes in it, taken from Walter's Object Drawing, shows how shading of double curved surfaces is being done in freehand pen work. This method of shading is sometimes used in draughting to represent objects having irregular or broken surfaces, such as rough cut stone or carved wood, while stippling is used for smooth surfaces like paper, leather, unpolished metal, etc. Fig. 68, belonging to the course of advanced freehand drawing, is reprinted here for comparison only, and is not to be copied.

Draw the plate twice as high and wide, i. e., four times as large as the given original.

Draw a neat border line.

Write an inscription in the upper left corner, using the *round writing* letter.

Add your signature in the lower left corner.

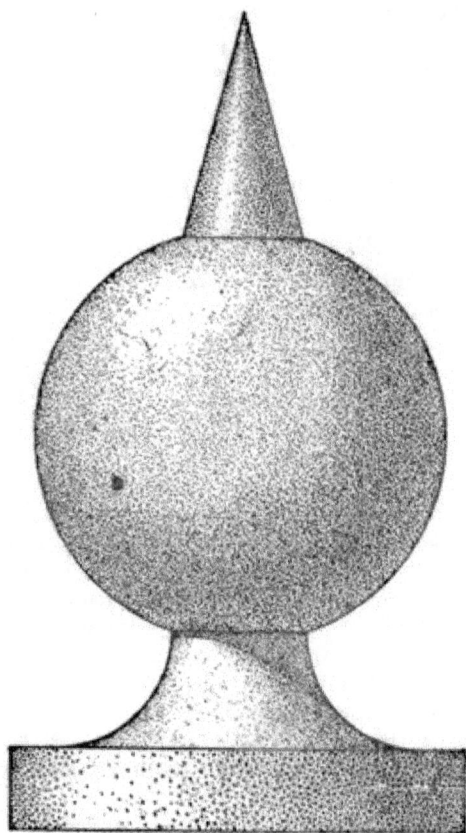

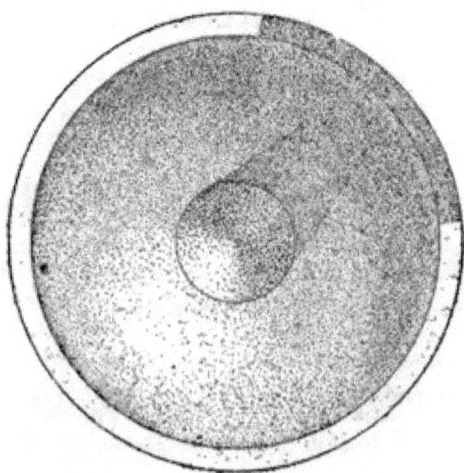

52. Shaded Isometric Projections.

PLATE IV. This plate is to be given to shading of isometric projections. There will be two figures, to be drawn as follows:

Figure A is to be an enlarged copy of the given cubical frame; side, 2¼ inches.

Figure B is to represent an isometric cube having a side of 1¼ inches. Upon each face draw a square pyramid having an axis of 1½ inches and a base of 1 inch.

Ink the visible outline of both figures and erase all non-visible parts.

FIG. 71.

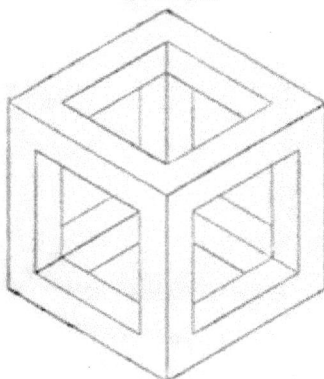

Shade the edges dividing light from dark faces, assuming the light to come from the left and above.

Shade all faces to right by strong tintlines placed close. All shaded faces but two of the second figure, will be vertical and must be shaded by vertical tint lines. The two faces in the second figure, which are not vertical, are the right faces of the top and bottom pyramids. These are to be shaded in the direction of the altitude of the face triangles.

Ink the border line.
Add an inscription.
Sign your name.

53. Plan of a Homelot.

PLATE V. This plate is to consist of an enlarged copy of figure 72 (adopted, with some alterations, from Prof. W. R. Ware's Examples of Building Construction).

The given plan is drawn to a scale of 1 inch to 32 feet, but the copy is to be drawn four times as large, i. e., to a scale of 1:192. Remember that *plane figures are to each other as the squares of homologous lines.*

Turn the plan around so that north will be above and south below, which is the usual position of a landscape plan. Sketch the roads and the outlines of the tree-clumps in pencil, measuring all positions by *triangulation* from the base line. Finish the former with hard-rubber

curve and drawing pen, and draw the latter freehand, using the
writing pen. Notice how the shading of the clumps and ground on the
east gives relief and naturalness to the lawn.

Draw a border line.

FIG. 72

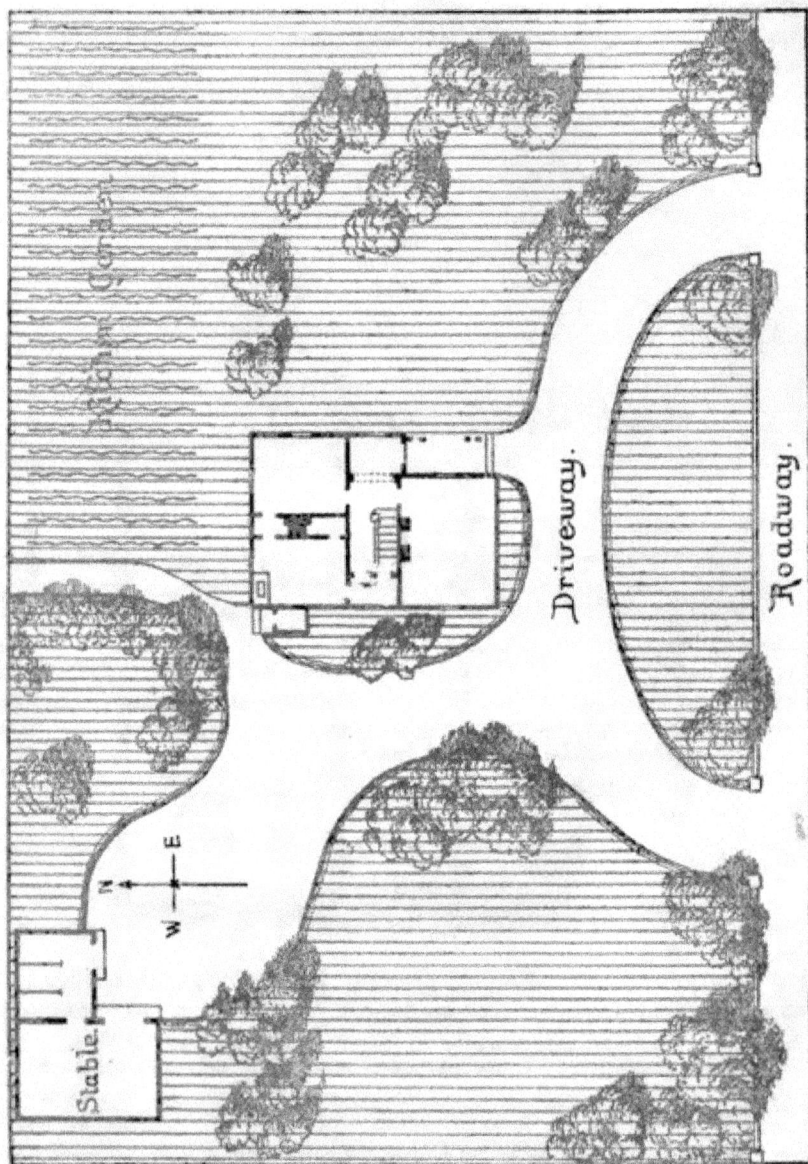

Add a neat inscription, " Homelot " over the plan. This may be drawn in the simple and easily sketched Egyptian letter, but it should not be enlarged, and the letters should be placed close together.

In the left corner, below, write in small, but neat letters, "Scale 1 Inch to 16 Feet."

In the right corner sign your name.

54. A Floor Plan.

PLATE VI. **This plate** is to consist of an enlarged copy of the given floor plan (taken, with some alterations, from Soennecker's Textbook **on** Round Writing.)

The given plan is drawn to the scale of 1 inch **to 16 feet. Make the** copy four times as large, i. e., to the scale of 1 inch **to 8 feet.**

FIG. 73.

Ground Plan

Plastered partitions on studs are assumed to be 6 inches in thick. ness, half partitions on each side of a sliding door, 3 inches; and the space for the sliding door, 3 inches. Brick walls are usually made 12 inches in thickness. The line outside the wall represents the watertable, a stone band even with the floor, which projects about 2 inches. Door openings are left blank, and windows are shown by 3 lines connecting two squares that represent boxjambs and are partly inserted in the brick walls.

After copying this floor plan it would be good practice for the student to draw a set of floor plans of his home, from measurements taken by himself. This would give him, in addition, an insight into the work of architectural construction, which mere copying of plans and eleva- tions cannot give.

All inscriptions should be horizontal, straight, plain and small. There should be no attempt at fancy work of any kind.

Always add scale and signature to mechanical drawings of this kind.